ANYTHING FROM A PIN TO AN ELEPHANT

Tales of Norfolk Retail

CHRIS ARMSTRONG

AMBERLEY

First published 2016

Amberley Publishing
The Hill, Stroud
Gloucestershire, GL5 4EP

www.amberley-books.com

British Library Cataloguing in Publication Data.
A catalogue record for this book is available from the British Library.

ISBN: 978 1 4456 5652 6 (print)
ISBN: 978 1 4456 5653 3 (ebook)

Typesetting and Origination by Amberley Publishing.
Printed in the UK.

ANYTHING FROM A PIN TO AN ELEPHANT

Tales of Norfolk Retail

Contents

Acknowledgements

I would like to record my thanks to the many who have cheerfully allowed me access to archives and provided me with so much additional information. In particular I should like to express my gratitude to Richard Jarrold, Caroline Jarrold, Michael Baker, Anthony Baker, Paul Roy, Bruce Sturrock, Tim Aldiss, Tim Summers, and to Lesley Leigh, Sue Billings and Peter Dormer of Break who have been so generous with their time. Also I should like to thank Ken Taylor for permitting the use of his picture of the premises of Bakers of Holt.

Almost all the images in this book have been sourced either from the respective businesses or from members of the families concerned, each of whom has consented to their publication, or from postcards or prints of such antiquity that it has not proved practical to identify any copyright owner. In the case of the chapter on Break, where the illustrations include individual volunteers or members of staff, the charity has confirmed that those concerned have consented to their use. The remaining images were photographed by the author.

Introduction

The popularity of recent television drama series' such as *The Paradise* and *Mr Selfridge*, and the splendid three-part documentary by Dr Pamela Cox, *Shop Girls: the True Story of Life Behind the Counter*, is evidence enough of the level of public interest in the history of the retail trade.

It might be seen as an irony that such interest has become manifest just as the pendulum seems to be swinging inexorably away from traditional stores towards convenience shopping by use of the internet. Today, it is possible to obtain all manner of goods without stirring from one's home. The attractions are clear – no travelling, no parking problems, no crowded counters, no struggling with parcels – just a click of the mouse and the goods are delivered to your door.

The increased interest in traditional stores is perhaps more than just nostalgia. Shopping can be fun; some have even claimed it is therapeutic. As with so many things, it seems that it is only when people recognise that they may lose something that they begin fully to appreciate it; I would argue that such is the case with traditional retail outlets, and, in particular, the department store.

In Norfolk we are astonishingly lucky; even today we have a remarkable collection of genuinely independent stores which have overcome just about everything that has been thrown at them. They have experienced wars, bombs, fires, recessions and depressions, family fallings out, takeover bids and a succession of revolutionary changes in their market which have shifted the tectonic plates of the retail industry to a degree unimaginable to their founders.

That, so far at least, these stores have met every challenge, maintained their independence and, indeed that they still exist at all, is a tribute to the imagination, the determination and the resilience of successive generations of a handful of remarkable retailing families. We should celebrate their achievements.

Norfolk has always 'done different'. It has spawned some splendidly iconic – and sometimes eccentric – retailers. Many no longer exist. Rumsey Wells (hatters) early neighbours of Jarrolds in Cockey Lane, proudly proclaimed that their caps were 'the most expensive in the world' but finally closed in the 1970s after nearly 160 years of supplying headgear to suit every whim and fashion. Chamberlins, founded in 1814, and a department store of over 40,000 square feet, was, at the start of the twentieth century, a fine example of modern retailing. Centrally heated, lit by chandeliers, and with huge internal Corinthian columns, it was the epitome of contemporary chic, but by the 1950s was in the ownership of Marshall & Snellgrove. Today its fine premises are occupied by Tesco. Others have survived but not as independent stores. The much loved Bonds and Curls are still in their original sites, but as part of John Lewis and Debenhams, respectively.

What is it which marks out as different the stores covered in this book? There seem to be some common characteristics, but a number of differences too. Strength of character would seem a prerequisite for survival. One can find immensely strong characters in the history of each store, but not necessarily in every generation. Imagination, adaptability and drive are clearly seen in the management of each. Some founding families seem to have worked in harmony through each succeeding generation; others have found it necessary to manoeuvre among themselves to maintain their businesses.

In one case, Bakers & Larners of Holt, a group of splendidly Wodehousian aunts, who between them comprised the entire board in some of the interwar years, fell out with each other so badly that their squabbles had to be resolved in the High Court with Kings Counsel appearing for each side. The next generation couldn't agree about much either, and the success of the company today would not have been possible without a concordat among the three cousins who succeeded them, an agreement perhaps easier to achieve because, although all three contributed significantly, only one, Michael Baker, was prepared to take up an executive role.

The only other case in which family disagreements have been so apparent was that of the Jarrold family, and that was nearly a century earlier when the relationship between John Jarrold (II) and his three surviving sons deteriorated so badly that the two generations would only communicate with each other in writing.

John Jarrold (II) was a remarkable and strong person, but perhaps the most interesting character of all was Arnold Roy, one of the founding brothers of Roys of Wroxham. He was a man of exceptional imagination with an extraordinary gift for self-publicity, which made him a national figure. Hailed as 'the Norfolk Napoleon' in the press, an extraordinary appearance on the BBC's *In Town Tonight* in the 1930s gave rise to an avalanche of letters from ladies wishing to marry him! Some of these are still in the Roys archives, and they provided some of the most entertaining elements of the research to write this book.

Perhaps the most rewarding piece of research was to be found at Palmer's of Great Yarmouth. Their archive yielded an absolute gem – the book of rules laid down for the housekeeper responsible for looking after those members of staff who lived over the store. No account I have seen published of the lives of such staff comes anywhere near as close to creating an understanding of what their life was really like. This comprehensive list of instructions governs virtually every aspect of their lives: what they ate, who carved and who sat where while they did, what they could drink, what happened in ill health, and what to do if 'followers' were at the back door. The detail is amazing, even down to the differing thickness of the slices of bread to be provided for male and female staff.

In almost every story there are examples of the operation of the law of unintended consequences. The most recent of these was in the case of Aldiss of Fakenham. In the 1980s Tim Aldiss came up with a new plan to encourage customers to come to the store.

He invited a Tarot card reader to tell the fortune of each customer. Customers loved it and queued for hours to have a turn. It was so successful that the event had to be extended to enable all of those, at least one of whom had driven 100 miles for the privilege, to hear their fortunes. Tim Aldiss had expected there to be great interest locally, and he was not disappointed. But he hadn't bargained for national press coverage and radio interviews from as far away as New Zealand. It wasn't so much the initiative itself which attracted the attention but the reaction of the local Baptist minister who characterised the event as 'devil worship' and whose congregation threatened a boycott of the store.

It has been great fun researching these stores; I have come to admire both the resilience of the current generation and their forebears and the imaginative methods they have deployed to keep ahead in the retail revolution of the last few years.

There is just one more story in this book. I have referred in the book to the massive changes in the retail market over the last thirty or forty years, from out of town centres to the rapid advance of the internet. One other development has been the arrival of charity shops, their expansion being fuelled during the recession by the availability of premises at low cost.

In Norfolk we have seen many such shops open. One local charity in particular, Break, has been in the forefront of this growth. And here I must disclose a personal interest: I was for ten years a Trustee of this charity and for three of them Chairman of its Board. But it earns its place entirely on merit. For a local charity to grow its shop portfolio to over fifty, the vast majority in Norfolk and neighbouring counties, is a remarkable achievement, and a story well worth the telling in a celebration of all that is best in the Norfolk retail scene.

Chris Armstrong
Bodham
June 2015

The Remarkable Story of the Roys of Wroxham

Anything from a pin to an elephant
> Arnold Roy, Joint Founder of Roys of Wroxham when asked
> on the BBC's *In Town Tonight* in April 1938 what could be bought at his store.

Partial family tree of the Roy family showing the relationship of those mentioned in this chapter

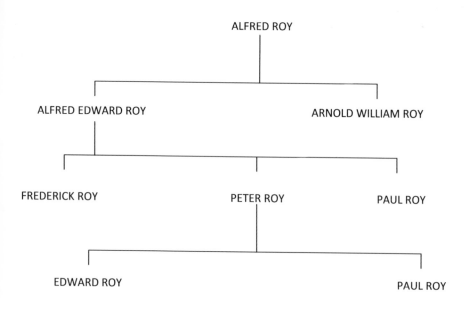

Wroxham, *c*. 1908 from an old postcard.

In the middle of the nineteenth century Wroxham was little more than a hamlet, with a population of around 350. By the 1890s the population had grown only to 400, but the character of the village was changing fast. Payne Jennings, the Victorian photographer, published a book about Norfolk in 1892. The written commentary to his picture of Wroxham Bridge described how it was quite usual to see thirty or more yachts moored there to top up their supplies at the butcher's shop or one of the two general stores. And this was just the beginning.

The key to the change in Wroxham's character is to be found, as so often, in the development of the railway, and soon it was to become the 'Capital of the Broads'. This change offered the opportunity for men of initiative to establish new businesses and there were several who did do. One was John Loynes, a Norwich carpenter with an enthusiasm for yachting and the skill to build his own boat, which he based at Wroxham. Soon people were asking whether they could hire his boat and, alive to the opportunity, he built more. Moving his business to Wroxham in around 1890, he went into the chartering business in a much bigger way. He recognised that some people wanted more than just a day's sailing and he began to build yachts with sleeping facilities, beginning a fashion which continues to this day.

The clientele were not just local, those trains which brought the rich and fashionable to Cromer stopped at Wroxham, and it became the thing to take a boating holiday en route, creating a demand for more luxurious boating accommodation. The railways that brought the holidaymakers had also diminished the need for Norfolk's traditional trading wherries, and soon these were being converted for holiday use. Press Bros of North Walsham were at the forefront of this development, offering 'Wherry yachts', the *Bertha*, the *Lucy*, the *Elsie*, the *Kate*, and the *Diligent*. These were fitted out to luxurious standards, rented out with a crew of two to sail the boat and to look after the hirer's every whim. Separate sleeping cabins for Ladies and Gentlemen were provided, that of the Gentlemen being twice as large as that for the Ladies but converted in daytime to a 'dining saloon' in which the party could enjoy the meals prepared by the crew. Each cabin had its own private lavatory. However, even in yachts as capacious as these the conditions must have been fairly cramped. Four ladies were accommodated in their cabin, measuring 9 feet by 7 feet, and equipped with washstand, lockers and the inevitable – and of course, absolutely essential – mirror. The gentlemen, up to six of them, had double the space but the centre of the cabin was taken up by the long dining table. One mystery is where the space was found for the piano, which was an optional extra!

These developments created an opportunity for someone with an entrepreneurial spirit to build a significant business. In the brothers Alfred and Arnold Roy, Wroxham soon found they had two. Together they built what, by the 1930s, had come to be known as 'The Largest Village Store in the World'.

Above left: Arnold Roy, joint founder of the store.

Above right: Alfred Roy, joint founder of the store.

The brothers were the sons of Alfred (Snr) the village carpenter at Reepham, who also ran the village store, so retail was in the brothers' blood. Only two years apart in age, they were very different in character, although they got on well. Fortunately their skills were complementary.

The elder, Alfred, had his feet firmly on the ground. He was to bring thoughtfulness, common sense and stability to the partnership, all underlaid with a determination to succeed. Arnold was a different character, a remarkable self-publicist, but one with great flair, great ambition and extraordinary drive. He was a CHARACTER; he would have been disappointed if the word were not in capitals.

In later years Arnold delighted in telling the story of how, at the age of fourteen, he had been given a donkey, had built a cart for it to pull, filled the cart with oranges and other goods from his father's shop and taken to the hamlets around Reepham to make a few pennies. It was an early sign of things to come. When they grew up Alfred worked first at Blickling Mill before moving on to London, while Arnold headed straight for the bright lights. It was no Dick Whittington story: he earned just a shilling per day as a warehouse boy, an income he supplemented by opening the doors of the hansom cabs of shoppers, or taking the reins of their horses as they shopped at the big stores. No shrinking violet and always willing to add a romantic dimension to the story of his success, Arnold later attributed his retail ambitions to a conviction forged at this time that he could do as well, or better than, the proprietors of the stores outside whose doors he earned pennies in tips.

In 1895 Arnold's sharp eye spotted an opportunity when a shop in Coltishall became available. In those days Coltishall was a thriving community, an important centre of the maltings industry; in 1881 its population of approaching 2,000 enjoyed the services of four pubs and two other beer retailers. Arnold approached his father for a loan to set him up, and Alfred (Snr) agreed on condition that the business was run by both sons, and their sister Katie. His elder daughter, Julia, was already living in Aylsham and was working as a teacher. The store also operated as a post office, Alfred becoming postmaster and Arnold managing the shop. They were ambitious, and promptly looked to establish new branches. First on their list was Dereham, not an obvious choice as it was around 25 miles distant, but it was, at that time, a thriving town. This was quickly followed with a new addition closer to Coltishall, at Hoveton St John on the edge of Wroxham.

This was a tiny store but, as became the way with Roys, it made a big claim – to be 'Universal Providers'. A Mr Carver was appointed manager but soon Arnold moved over to take control himself. He had recognised the opportunities offered by the expanding holiday market. Some were sad to see Mr Carver go. His customers got up a petition for his reinstatement but Arnold still took control, leaving Alfred and Katie at Coltishall. Katie married in 1901 and moved away to Fakenham where, with her husband, she put the knowledge she had acquired to good use, as they opened their own shop. Meanwhile, the business at Wroxham grew rapidly as boating holidays became ever more popular with customers who liked to arrive at their boats to find provisions already on board. Roys offered such a service for more than sixty years, later sending out catalogues running to 150 pages, from which the customer could select whatever they wanted and find it waiting for them on board. And it wasn't just provisions; by the

Roys' first store in Wroxham, 1899.

1920s they were even providing radios for use on board at £1 a week and gramophones (complete with a selection of twenty-four 'double-sided' records) for 12/6d. Devotees of Arthur Ransome will be reminded of 'The Hullabaloos' who so upset the members of the Coot Club.

Roys were moving ever closer to matching that claim of being 'Universal Providers'. Soon, almost the only item Arnold Roy didn't stock was a bushel under which to hide his light; he was a self-publicist of almost Olympian proportions. It wasn't just vanity, although there is evidence enough to suggest that he revelled in his public image. His efforts were deliberately aimed at making the name of Roys as widely known as possible, and they succeeded brilliantly. Roys started, both nationally and even internationally, to punch well above its weight.

Arnold kept a scrapbook in which he collected press cuttings about himself and the store. The range of publications in which he featured was immense. The most geographically distant was the *Sunday Times* of Johannesburg, which described the store, in 1935, as being 'as big as any three of the largest general stores in Johannesburg put together'. Supplying hire boats was still a key part of the Roys offering, and the South African reporter was less impressed with the hirers who were Roys customers:

some of the most amazing freaks in England seem to find pleasure in boating. Men who look like vegetarians, with beards like dyed vermicelli, with khaki shirts and shorts and knapsacks take in the delights of Wroxham through horn-rimmed glasses. Women, sometimes abnormally broad in the beam, stuff white silken blouses into the waists of blue serge bellbottomed trews. They carry walking sticks and smoke cigarettes at the slightest provocation.

Cover of Roys' boating catalogue, 1930s.

Arnold's 'rags to riches' story featured in *The Fish Traders Gazette*, *The Grocer's Gazette*, *The Ironmonger*, *Men's Wear*, *The British Baker*, *The Draper's Record* and *The Motor Cycle and Cycle Trader*. With the occasional embellishment, all told the same story about the donkey and the oranges, the looking after hansoms and horses outside London stores, the self-belief and the success bought with hard honest toil. Sometimes they would end with a little homily from Arnold on the virtues of self-improvement – he was the new Samuel Smiles. But he wasn't content with the trade press – that might raise his standing within the trade, but he had bigger fish to fry than the readers of *The Fish Traders Gazette*. He courted the national press; *The Daily Express* reported, in 1939, that he had 'built a village store into a business with a £250,000 turnover' and its Sunday counterpart that he had 'bought 5 private saloon cars, with chauffeurs' to pull in shoppers from outlying villages. The *Reynolds News* described him as 'The Norfolk Napoleon'; he was featured in *Tit-Bits* and *The Star* reported in 1939 that he employed 800 staff, roughly the equivalent number employed by Roys in 2014, though some of the latter are part-time.

Of course, the First World War had had an impact. The Dereham store was closed in 1914, never to reopen, and the premises leased to the International Stores, its manager, a Mr Frostick, having been called up to fight. Alfred (Snr) died the following year and his Reepham store closed. The two brothers were occupied with running the remaining stores, but in 1916 Arnold was also called up, at the age of forty-two. The following year Alfred (Jnr) married and expanded his interests into farming in addition to managing the business.

After the war the business grew rapidly. As was the case with so many firms, a problem arose when staff returned from fighting to find others doing the jobs they had had before the War. One such was Edmund Newstead who could find no vacancy in Roys ironmongery, where he had worked before. The brothers were still keen to expand, and to get nearer to living up to that 'Universal Provider' tag and they decided to buy a bakery in Coltishall as an additional business, appointing Newstead its first manager. In time the decision to buy that bakery was to prove of immense value to the wider business, as will become apparent.

During 'the roaring twenties', Arnold entered energetically into the spirit of the age with a programme of public dances held in the shop's premises. Special buses were laid on to bring patrons from Norwich and other towns to a series of 'Pyjama Dances' at one shilling and sixpence a head or more decorous 'Radio dances' at a shilling. Attendances in excess of 1,000 were not unusual. Similar audiences attended concerts, and he extended these to include religious music, such concerts starting at 8.00 p.m. on a Sunday so as not to depress the size of local evensong congregations. Of course, there were other benefits: not only did these events bring people in but they offered the opportunity to show off new lines. The radio was a particular case in point. At an early stage Arnold, an inveterate sloganeer, had come up with the phrase 'a wireless set in every cottage'. As usual his promotional activities were distinctly left field. In 1924 he hung speakers over the branches of an oak tree outside the shop so the public could hear the broadcast chimes of Big Ben, followed by a concert, all advertised widely in advance. Following this he issued a press statement headed 'Big Ben heard in Wroxham' and, delighted with the public response, continued to provide the service.

ROYS' DANCES

To assist local Charities and to provide funds for
the seating accommodation of 5,000 spectators
at the next Wroxham Water Carnival, 1929

the management of

ROYS' DANCES, WROXHAM BRIDGE

announce

GRACEFUL
PYJAMA
DANCING

... ON ...

Saturday, Sept. 22

8 till 12

M.C.: Mr. W. LeNEVE PAINTER

Pyjama Dance at 11 o'clock precisely, in two classes,
competitors only to take the floor.

CLASS A. — PARTNERS in Pyjamas, to be judged as **PARTNERS**
CLASS B. — DANCERS in Pyjamas, to be judged **INDIVIDUALLY**

Dressing Rooms for Competitors

PRIZES

CLASS A. — 1st and 2nd Prizes for Dancing Partners wearing the choicest
and best-matched Suits.

CLASS B. — 1st and 2nd Prizes for Dancers wearing Pyjama Suits best
decorated with Broadland features such as windmills, bridges,
yachts, birds, etc.

Order of the Dance

That the event may be judged and viewed to the best advantage, the dance will
consist of two minutes each of : **Valeta, Fox Trot, Boston Two-step** and **Valse**

What could be nicer than to see this choice array of Boudoir Dress elegantly
displayed at 11 o'clock?

2 Lucky Number Tickets at the Door.

Admission 1/6.   LATE BUS FOR NORWICH.

Last Saturday's attendance over 400.

THE MOST POPULAR DANCE of the District, and all the sur-
plus proceeds for the next Wroxham Water Carnival, which
supports local Charities.

C. R. Chamberlin, Printer, Wroxham.

Poster advertising a Roys' Pyjama Dance, 1920s.

Poster for Roys' Radio Dance and Concert of sacred music.

All this activity radically increased the traffic in the village so, having already provided the community with street lighting, litter bins and public lavatories, he decided to manage the traffic as well. He employed a retired policeman, Sergeant Page, dressed him in a constable's uniform and placed him on point duty by the store. Sadly, the chief constable was not amused and put an end to the initiative.

For those unable to travel to Wroxham, Roy's had always provided roundsmen – indeed part of the business logic for buying the bakery had been the additional rounds this provided. In the early days these rounds had been carried out using a pony and cart, but now with mechanisation Arnold struck a good bargain, buying a fleet of former Royal Mail vans. Rebranding them was easy – just remove the '..al Mail' from the lettering on the side, add an 's' and the vans were branded 'Roys' – no need to repaint them, their original red and gold could become the corporate colours! Roys were early exponents of the loss leader. Roundsmen always carried at least one item to be sold at cost, an early statement that Roys aimed to compete on price, as they have ever since.

But the 1920s were not just an era when flappers with bobs and shingles charlestoned or black bottomed around the store in pyjamas – sadly there seems no photographic record of those events, though Arnold's scrapbook provides evidence that, although he remained single, he was attracted to the opposite sex. His early days in London had been towards

A FEW WELL-KNOWN TROJAN VAN USERS.

A typical Roys' van of the 1920s and 1930s.

'Policeman' on point duty outside Roys' stores.

the end of the era of the 'professional beauty' when likenesses of Lillie Langtry, Patsy Cornwallis West and others were sold in their thousands, and he maintained the tradition, including contemporary 'pin-ups' cut from the newspapers among his other cuttings. It was also the decade of the General Strike and Arnold, as with most things, saw this as an opportunity. Proudly declaring that 'so long as there is food, the public shall have it from Roys', he despatched a fleet of cars and vans to the markets of London to ensure there was ample stock. Not content with this he decided to take a leaf out of Churchill's book and produce a daily newssheet. A somewhat faded copy of one edition is carefully pasted into his scrapbook. A cyclostyled print, familiar in style to all those who were still using the Gestetner duplicating system right up until the 1970s, it contained everything from weather forecasts to revised travel arrangements as well as news. It was called the *Roys Press*, edited by Arnold Roy. While it was an undoubted public service there are echoes of Baden Powell who, during the siege of Mafeking, actually produced postage stamps bearing his own image and published the *Mafeking Mail*, a similar newsletter with the slogan 'Issued Daily, Shells Permitting'.

While Arnold was busy promoting both the store and himself, Alfred was working away in Coltishall, expanding both the premises and the range of goods. By 1927 the store had doubled in size, and the post office had been moved into adjoining premises. With Roys Bakery also going strong, the brothers were a significant presence in both Coltishall and Wroxham, and Alfred moved them nearer to that 'Universal Providers' tag by opening both men's and women's outfitters as well as stepping up the scale of the grocery store.

Wroxham, 1934, with Roys' dominating the town centre.

Unlike Arnold, who remained single, Alfred had married and had a family of four. He had interests and commitments outside the business as a parent and as a councillor, and he had developed an interest in farming. At Wroxham, too, a new food hall was opened in 1927.

In 1931 the brothers decided to change from a partnership to limited company status. In doing so they made two decisions which were to have a major impact on the company more than twenty years later. First they decided, against advice, that all the shares should be split equally between them. They had always rubbed along well together, and saw no reason to establish the company on a basis which would, either by giving a majority of the shares to one of them, or by involving a third shareholder with a small parcel of shares, avoid any risk of stalemate in the event of a profound disagreement between them about the direction of the company. Second, they decided to leave the booming bakery out of the equation and continue to operate that business as partners.

For the moment, though, things carried on as before; the bakery continued to grow and, although the Coltishall store was becoming less important than that at Wroxham this was a reflection of growth at the latter rather than any diminution at the former, which continued its steady development. But given the growing significance of both the store and the village, it seemed sensible to move the company's headquarters to Wroxham.

Arnold had, like his brother, become involved in community matters. He became both a parish and a district councillor, but in 1935 he was appointed a magistrate. Again his scrapbook told the story; in it are letters of congratulation on the latter appointment, while the pleasure he took in his eventual election as a councillor is evident from the annotated election notices he pasted in. In the 1930s he was also chairman of the Wroxham Advancement Association. In the latter capacity he crossed swords with T. R. C. Blofeld (father of Henry Blofeld the cricket commentator). Arnold's disagreement with Mr Blofeld on the question of public access to Hoveton Broad was a matter of public record; they stood against each other in two local council elections. The result was a one all draw and Arnold would seem to have been delighted when he scored the equaliser. When the writer was himself a magistrate, there were photographs in the retiring room of distinguished former magistrates, including one of Mr Blofeld, whose other son became a judge. If Blofeld and Arnold ever sat in court together one imagines that the conversation in the retiring room between cases would have been quite entertaining for the third member of the bench.

Aside from his civic responsibilities, Arnold continued to attract attention like iron filings to a magnet, coining slogans at the drop of a hat. He stocked 'everything from a top-sail to a tin opener; from a mainsail to a match' reported *Town & Country Magazine*. His ambition was 'to bring Harrods to Wroxham' he claimed. Perhaps the slogan that became best known was his assertion that 'at Roys you can buy anything from a pin to an elephant'. This was probably not original; Arnold may have heard the term while in London as it has also been attributed to the founders of Whiteley's and of Harrods.

He made this claim when he was interviewed on the wireless in the BBC programme *In Town Tonight* in April 1938. There were repercussions: he subsequently received an order for a lion cub! Anxious as always to satisfy customer demands, and with a wide-open eye on the press, Arnold negotiated with possible suppliers and produced a livestock price list which included Rhesus Monkeys at £1. 8s 0d, a pair of small bear cubs at £24, an African

Mongoose at £3, a 'Grand Cock Singing Canary' for 12/6d, a tame adult leopard at £35, and white mice at 4d each. The customer who enquired about a lion cub was offered a choice of two, either a 'fine cub, perfect' at £16, or one which 'has had rickets, not a good cub, bow legs, heavy in front – alright if on show by itself', a snip at a fiver. Whether the customer bought either, or whether his enquiry was just a joke is not on record. At least Arnold had demonstrated his commitment to truth in advertising.

In his broadcast Arnold also claimed that he had everything he wanted in life, except a wife. This was a reprise of an earlier magazine interview but this time it was widely reported in the press and resulted in a host of interesting offers. Some of these letters are in a file in the Roys' archive – generally they are rather sad and vary from the bold to the very modest 'writing on behalf of a friend' variety. One must have tickled his fancy particularly because it joined the other documents in his scrapbook. In the broadcast much had been made of his commercial success. He was, by then, routinely described as a millionaire in the press. A lady from Hertfordshire sought to make an asset out of her own poverty, her letter beginning,

Dear Sir, I have read about you in the Daily Mirror - and that you are looking around for a wife, and I don't suppose you are looking for a woman of money or rank, as you have enough of your own.

How seriously one should take Arnold's assertion about marriage is debatable. While his interest in pretty girls is evident in the scrapbook he also glued in a press report of a talk by Dr Bernard Hollander, a phrenologist and psychologist who claimed that there were 'eighteen reasons why men fail, but mainly marriage'. Warming to his theme, Hollander went on to ascribe the majority of failures by men to 'the nagging wife, the clinging wife, the domineering wife, the dull-witted wife who is something of a millstone'. The obituary on his death in 1934 doesn't disclose whether the good doctor was himself married or not. One imagines that if he were, then his views might have encouraged his wife to produce a whole host of new bumps for him to read, if only with the help of a mirror.

Under all the bluster there was a serious side to Arnold as well. He contributed to *The Retailers Compendium*, a bible for those in the business. Paul Roy recalls that when he was studying retail at university in the 1990s, the compendium, complete with Great Uncle Arnold's contribution, was still a standard work used in the course. Professionally Arnold was forward thinking. He introduced an outbound telephone sales service as early as the 1930s; calls were made to existing customers to advise them of new lines. His philosophy was straightforward: success was the result of thrift, honesty, hard work and common sense. 'There is no corner on success' he once said, 'it is always up at auction and the one who pays the most for it in energy and grit gets it.' The use of the auction analogy was probably not accidental. By now, Arnold had added another string to the Roys bow; he had set up a valuation and auctioneering business. Judging by the crowds in an early photograph of him conducting an al fresco auction, he pulled in the punters, probably attracted as much by his patter as by the lots.

Throughout the 1930s the business continued to expand; all seemed set fair. In was in the same decade that Roys was first called 'The World's Largest Village Store'. Tradition has it that the accolade was earned in a competition, but there seems to be no record

Arnold Roy conducting an auction.

1930s Roys' advertisement.

to confirm this in the company's archives. Be that as it may, the claim has never been successfully challenged. By 1937 the expansion was such that *The Sunday Graphic* mused that to 'walk down Wroxham's main street you have to dodge to miss Roy's vans, and his lamp posts – all the street lighting is provided by him'.

Still significant in the expansion was the business with the hire boats. The hire companies appreciated Roys as much as did their customers. At this time the companies used Roys exclusively to stock their craft. It was said that on all the boats hired from Wroxham, every cup, plate, blanket and primus stove had been supplied by Roys. Way back in 1912, when Roys first set up an ironmongery department they had employed a Hubert Newstead to manage it; he was still in the same role nearly fifty years later. He was reportedly responsible in the 1930s for an idea which has been a boon to Broads boat users ever since. Because of the muddy bottom of the Broads traditional anchors were ineffective and Newstead devised the now ubiquitous mudweight.

For all this growth, the health of the business was not as robust as it appeared. The expansion had not been matched by improvements in the administrative systems. Sales targets went unmonitored, there was no clear system for assessing profitability, the staff had grown significantly, and so had 'shrinkage'. Management information was sketchy and unreliable. Alfred became uneasy. He understood that the administrative and financial skills of the brothers, while adequate for a small business, were stretched too far by the size to which Roys had grown. These shortcomings were made worse by the death of a competent senior member of the management and Alfred decided that the time had come to acquire additional expertise, especially in financial matters; he proposed that an accountant should be employed so that decisions could be based on accurate information. Arnold did not agree. His was a nature that didn't welcome too much detailed analysis. His strength was as a 'big picture' man, and it was that very talent which had been largely responsible for the success so far.

This disagreement between the brothers, apparently the first of significance, brought sharply into focus the mistake they had made when taking 50 per cent of the shares each on converting from a partnership to a limited company. Alfred was sure they needed to employ professional expertise to keep the company healthy, and Arnold was adamant that they did not. There could only be one outcome, stalemate, and only one consequence, no change to the status quo. With the onset of the Second World War, there were enough other problems to deal with and no action was taken until after the war. By that time the situation was becoming critical, but in 1946 Alfred's eldest son, Fred, was demobbed and came to join the firm. He had been trained in retail in Kettering before the war and now, at twenty-six, he was back to stay. He started in Coltishall with his father, where he soon discovered the result of those deficiencies his father had identified a decade earlier. By now these were having a bigger impact and Fred quickly saw that something needed to be done, and soon. The administrative processes were clearly not effective: the premises were deteriorating and pilfering was rampant. Only the bakery in Coltishall, still the subject of a separate partnership, seemed immune from the problems – it had grown rapidly through the war years, producing almost 10,000 loaves a day.

Looking back on the situation years later, Fred described how, on the death of Alfred, in 1951, things came to a head. Alfred left his shares equally to Fred and his three siblings,

Fred Roy.

Betty and twin brothers Peter and Paul. But the problems were made worse by the impact of Estate Duty – in those days levied on all estates in excess of £2,000. Alfred had been in the habit of only drawing enough profit to enjoy his farm and educate his children, the balance had been left in the business, and now the business had to pay out that money in order that Alfred's executors could pay the death duties. Raising the wind was not easy; the company's overdraft rocketed. Fred believed that Arnold hadn't even warned the bank when he wrote the cheque for something in the order of £20/£30,000 (around £800,000 in today's values).

Clearly a grip needed to be taken, and Fred was the man to do it. He immediately moved from Coltishall to the bigger store at Wroxham. His move was not welcomed by everyone, but the family had agreed how most effectively to split the various roles. Paul would replace Fred at Coltishall, and Peter would take over the bakery.

Change is never comfortable for those set in their ways, and Fred's arrival in Wroxham inevitably caused a flutter in the hen coop and ruffled a few complacent feathers. He investigated everything, radically tightened the reporting of management information, and achieved the twin results of a more effective basis for decision making and a resentful attitude on the part of those who had been comfortable under the old regime. Their attitude was no secret to him – it was only with difficulty that he found a perch in an empty room. As he expressed it he 'commandeered it' as an office. Another focus was on reducing the bad debts owed to the company, the collection of which had previously been less than robust. But, popular or not, he had a beneficial effect: the overdraft was brought down by more than £10,000 in short order. By this time Arnold was approaching eighty, and there is no clear evidence of how he reacted to these changes, but the decisive way in which he had dealt with settling Alfred's estate suggests he was as committed as ever to the success of the business.

Barely had the dust settled on this first crisis than a bigger one followed. In 1953 Arnold died too. Single, he had left his shares to a highly respected senior manager, Harry Frostick, who had not only been general manager at Wroxham but also a trusted confidant for many years, and a loyal and effective servant of the company. Roys had not just been his life but that of his siblings too. The eldest, Walter, had been the manager of the Dereham store, and another, Tom, had run the bakery. His other brother had worked with Arnold's sister Katie and her husband at their Fakenham shop.

The difficulties caused by Alfred's death were repeated on Arnold's, but the scale was even greater. Like Alfred, Arnold had only drawn from profits what he needed to live on but, without a family and a farm, he had needed to take less out of the profits, so the amount owed to his estate by the business was even higher. The family shareholders had no collateral to offer the bank, and this time more drastic measures were required if the money to buy the shares left to Mr Frostick who was a willing seller, and happy to retire, was to be found.

First the company started to sell its property assets. Dereham, still leased to the International Stores, went first and was quickly followed by non-key buildings in Wroxham including the public lavatories Roys had provided for the town – they fetched a peppercorn price from the local council, but Roys retained the right to buy the site back at the same price (1s) if the lavatories were ever closed. Other properties to go were a branch shop at Potter Heigham and part of the Coltishall property. But there was no chance that these disposals would generate enough capital. It was at this point that the significance, more than twenty years earlier, of leaving the bakery as a separate partnership asset became clear. The bakery had done so well that it was able to advance £10,000 to the company and, with this addition, there were sufficient funds to repay Arnold's estate. But Harry Frostick still owned half the shares – shares in a company which was still generating significant sales, but virtually no profit; Fred was still working hard to sort things out. Half the shares were held by Mr Frostick, and the other half were shared equally between Alfred's children. The shareholders agreed that something had to be done. The decision was to take expert advice, and a team of management consultants descended on the hive to take their share of the honey and recommend what they felt was the best course for the future. Their advice was unequivocal: sell the business.

The family shareholders were not impressed. If the company was doomed then the price would be negligible. If the company could be saved then why let someone else benefit? For Frostick the position was different. Not only did he want to retire but he needed cash to pay the duty on his inheritance. So the family declined to sell their shares and negotiated with Harry Frostick to buy his. Negotiations were protracted, and even when a price was agreed a means still needed to be found to pay it. By this time the company had a substantial overdraft of £48,000, equivalent to around £1.2 million today. The bank was hardly likely to help. The solution the family found eventually was to mortgage the main Wroxham premises, and by 1955 they were able to buy out Harry Frostick.

In death as in life, Arnold had exercised extraordinary influence on the affairs of the company he had set up with his siblings, with a loan from their father. Looking at Arnold's contribution, one can see two sides. He made mistakes, three major ones: setting up the company with a fifty/fifty share split, refusing to heed Alfred's warning in the late 1930s about the direction of the company, and in creating a chaotic situation which threatened the future of the company by his testamentary disposition. Without him Roys might have been solvent, but – and it is a huge 'but' – it would certainly have been a lot smaller. The influence of Arnold Roy was immense and the sheer scale of the business today would almost certainly not have been possible without his remarkable talent for getting noticed. And there was more to him than that. As *The Daily Express* reported in 1937, 'Arnold Roy has made a fortune by making people feel important'. For the most part as one magazine had recorded ten years earlier, his business was, at the time 'conducted on the most modern and efficient lines and creates contented customers, and a contented staff'. Surely we can forgive him for taking his eye of the administrative ball later.

Perhaps because Arnold died single and childless some of his personal effects are kept in a box in the Roys archive. The box contains items such as his tie-pin – flashy enough to have appealed to Philbrick, the mysterious butler in Waugh's *Decline and Fall* – his pipe, the case for his pince-nez, though not the pince-nez themselves, and his driving licence. Perhaps surprisingly for such a high-octane character, the only endorsement dates from April 1912, when he was fined 5s for 'driving a motor car at 9.30 p.m. on 24 March without keeping a lamp burning on the back of the car'. For a man who later drove round the county in a rather noticeable Buick that seems an extremely modest misdemeanour. Perhaps his later appointment as a magistrate moderated his driving.

The shareholders, by now all family, were determined that they would not repeat the mistakes that had led to the earlier stalemate, and to the lack of on tap professional advice. One of the twins, Paul, had decided when things were at their most bleak, to emigrate to Canada and planned to take no part in the business; though he retained the ordinary shares he had received from his father, he transferred his debenture shares to his mother. The bulk of the ordinary shares were split equally between Fred, Peter and Betty and all of the family held debenture shares (which carried no voting rights but would have enjoyed preferential treatment in the event of insolvency) were converted to ordinary shares. To provide professional advice, non-executive directors from the legal and accountancy professions were appointed, as was a representative from the mortgagee. The bakery became a separate private company in 1955.

The decks were now cleared to rebuild the business. A start had been made in that, under Fred's careful management, the overdraft had been substantially reduced, but there was still insufficient capital available to look to expansion, yet growth had always been the Roys way. One more asset was disposed of; it was inconsistent with the retail focus of the company as it comprised two wholesale businesses relating to food and to tobacco. The disposal of these brought in more than expected – the value of the stock in hand exceeded expectations. With stronger and more professional management, and with debt under control, things gradually improved. After five or six years there was confidence that things had been turned round. The time was ripe for new ideas, and Fred came up with them.

Peter Roy.

In the late 1950s Roys had hosted a team of Australians who were in this country promoting the sale of Australian products. What they told Fred about the changes in retailing over there interested and impressed him, and he decided to go and have a look for himself. So, in 1960 he travelled out to Australia, deciding to return via Canada. What he saw excited him, and he was confident that he had seen into the future.

Each place he visited in Australia, in Canada, and in a brief incursion into the United States made him more sure that to succeed shops had to accommodate the motorist. In Australia he had seen, in suburban Melbourne, the site of a planned out of town shopping centre called Chadstone which was in the course of erection. Today Chadstone claims to be the largest shopping centre in the southern hemisphere with over 500 shops; perhaps inevitably in Australia it is now known as 'Chaddy'. When Fred visited it was still being built, 100 acres of recent pasture land being put to novel use. His Australian hosts emphasised the need to provide onsite parking to enable customers conveniently to shop. Their ambitions were fulfilled: today the average footfall at Chaddy is around 70,000 per day; Fred was right to be impressed. Visiting cousins in Vancouver, he was taken across the border into the United States and saw examples of the finished product, thronged with shoppers whose cars were parked on the site. He moved on to see his brother in Toronto, and he was shown the same phenomenon. He returned to Wroxham absolutely convinced that Roys could emulate the success of these out of town centres. He was sure, too, that the status quo was not good enough. As he said in a later speech reviewing the business

'... 'Roys are still in business because we were prepared to change. Change is difficult for people, but we have changed and we should not have been in business still unless we were prepared to'.

In the same speech Fred described how he decided to replicate, on a smaller scale, Chadstone and turn Wroxham into an out-of-town centre for shoppers from Norwich. He had recognised that the whole retail sector was undergoing huge change as the nationals were beginning to play a much more aggressive game and the independents were suffering. Everything seems to go in circles – the breeze the nationals are feeling from continental discounters today is little different from that they themselves caused the independents to feel forty or fifty years ago.

Fred was alive to the dangers and alert to the means of trying to neutralise them. His out-of-town philosophy was key but Roys also had to be able to price competitively. At the time there was an organisation called Associated Departmental Stores, which operated on behalf of a number of independent stores, enabling them to have more muscle when negotiating with suppliers than they would as individual businesses. Later Fred became chairman of the organisation, known now as Associated Independent Stores.

Meanwhile the board members applied themselves to the task of developing the new type of store. At Chadstone the Australians only had to buy 100 acres of pasture from a local convent and build on a bare site. In Wroxham life was more difficult. Roads needed to be rerouted, as did the pipes for supplying water, gas and electricity, and extra land had to be acquired to create a site large enough to provide the car parking which was an essential element of the offering. All the hurdles, both practical and bureaucratic, were overcome in time for the store to be opened in July 1966 – just in time for the World Cup Final at Wembley at the end of the same month. The opening ceremony was performed by Fred and Peter's mother Florence, a charming tribute to the previous generation and a break from a tradition of celebrity openings such as that conducted earlier by George Formby; one would not have been surprised to learn, in the spirit of Arnold and, of course, through the press that Roys' had provided an extra lamp post for Formby to lean on while delivering his speech, under the ever-watchful eye of his wife, Beryl.

The new business model and changes in the market generally heralded the end of two traditional sources of sales for Roys. The long-standing business of supplying boat hirers was in steep decline. Holidaymakers were now arriving by car and were used to shopping in supermarkets. When they had been arriving by train, with little knowledge of local shops the Roys catalogue issued before their holiday had been invaluable, but now the service was becoming obsolete. Receipts were falling quickly and halved in the ten years to 1971, when it was closed. More serious was the decision about the future of the roundsmen who had been such an important part of Roys business for years. If the logic for driving the business forward was to make it easy for customers from outlying areas to visit the store, then there was little to commend continuing to service the same population with an expensive visiting sales service and it was discontinued in 1968. By then the turnover in such sales was low, running in absolute terms at around 60 per cent of what it had been in the 1930s; in real terms sales were barely 15 per cent of their peak. More significant still was that, with the success of the new store, the proportion of turnover derived from such sales had shrunk to a tiny percentage. They had to go,

George Formby opens a new department, under the watchful eye of his wife Beryl.

but not without some sadness at the ending of a long tradition. Roys had always been innovative and they had used the roundsmen to sell savings cards on which customers deposited 2s per week. Roys incentivised this by adding a penny to each shilling saved – an effective interest rate of over 8 per cent, which was a good deal for the customer and also for Roys who not only got their money in advance of the customer's purchase but also knew that the money deposited would be spent buying goods from them in the future. It is something of an irony that now, nearly fifty years later, some of the major nationals with whom Fred had been so keen to compete have, at a time when the population has aged so much and when public transport is less comprehensive, started their own delivery services to those in remote parts of the country. They had also started to open small 'convenience' stores, especially in town-centre locations. It shows just how difficult planning in the retail environment can be when social change necessitates such strategic changes.

The company was committed to the new strategy and soon opened a large food hall in Norwich. In the meantime the only delivery service still provided by Roys was for the bakery at Coltishall, and this was becoming uneconomic. The bakery had helped to save Roys in the 1950s but it was not a core business and the rounds were sold in 1973. Two years later it was clear that to continue to produce bread would require a substantial capital investment in new equipment and the business was sold. The rationale behind the expansion of the food business was first, a recognition that being able to compete on price required volume, and, second, that purchasers of low-margin food products might become customers for non-food lines which carried higher margins. Already, before the new food court in Norwich was opened that in Wroxham had been expanded.

While the business was growing, there were issues. Fred was approaching sixty and although Peter was five years younger, he had become heavily involved in the family farm. Succession planning was difficult because the next generation were still young and it was decided to go outside the family circle to find new senior management, if only as an interim measure until the next generation of the family were ready to take up the reins. Initially Brian Heron, an experienced manager, was recruited from Unilever in 1976 as deputy managing director. He recognised the nature of the issues facing the company, and that difficult decisions were called for; not having grown up as part of the Roys team, it was perhaps easier for him to focus on these. A major reorganisation was carried out with the objectives of trimming costs to the minimum and ramping up sales volumes. His method was to advertise aggressively and cut prices as far as possible, the loss of margin being compensated by the growth in volume. These principles remain a part of the Roys philosophy even today. Cost cutting inevitably meant significant reductions in staff numbers – Heron establishing a formula which related staff costs to a maximum percentage of sales. It was not popular, but it was effective: turnover by 1982 was six times that of five years earlier. Brian Heron was only with the company until 1978 when ill health led to his resignation. But the changes he had introduced were continued by Brian Godfrey who had, in the Heron era, been company secretary and after first joining the board as finance director became managing director, Fred Roy moving over to chairman.

In 1995 the company celebrated its centenary, and the celebrations were even more dramatic than planned. A commemorative window display was set alight overnight on the 6 May 1995 by a faulty spotlight and, despite a ten-hour fight involving numerous appliances to extinguish the blaze, the flagship building was razed to the ground. The resilience of the company was put to the test, and not for the first time. Way back in 1916 there had been a similar fire, but on that occasion the Norwich Fire Service had declined to attend, since the local parish council had failed to make the appropriate payment to secure their services! The board minutes of the then Norwich Union suggest that the claim was promptly settled at a cost of £300 – perhaps just an interim payment. Remarkably, after the 1995 fire the store was fully functional again in little more than a year.

As had been hoped at the time of Brian Heron's appointment the need to appoint the top executive team from outside the family proved temporary. Today the management of Roys is in the hands of Peter's sons, Ed and Paul. Both gained experience in retail with major stores before joining the firm and supplemented this with, in Ed's case, a qualification as a chartered accountant and in Paul's with an MBA. This combination of hands-on experience and specialist skills augurs well for the future of this remarkable family business in a challenging business environment. Arnold would have been proud that the business still thrives under family management and Alfred would have been just as glad that while the current generation demonstrate Arnold's flair, they have also acquired the qualifications and skills to overcome any obstacles they are met with. Today the company has eight branches: as well as Wroxham there are two outlets in Norwich and others in North Walsham, Dereham, Thetford, Beccles and Sudbury and has expanded its range to include a Garden Centre as well. The brothers face the future with confidence.

A Perlustration* of Palmer's of Great Yarmouth

*An archaic term meaning an investigation or review. Charles Palmer, a cousin of the founder of the store was the author of the huge and authoritative The *Perlustration of Great Yarmouth*.

Partial family tree of the Palmer family showing the relationship between those covered in this chapter

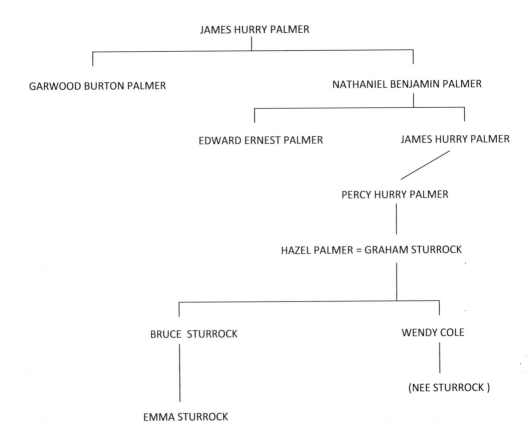

JAMES HURRY PALMER

GARWOOD BURTON PALMER

NATHANIEL BENJAMIN PALMER

EDWARD ERNEST PALMER

JAMES HURRY PALMER

PERCY HURRY PALMER

HAZEL PALMER = GRAHAM STURROCK

BRUCE STURROCK

WENDY COLE

(NEE STURROCK)

EMMA STURROCK

Palmers' store, dressed for the Jubilee in 1897.

1837 was an important year. Queen Victoria succeeded William IV and, in July, became the first monarch to move into Buckingham Palace. It was in the same year that Rowland Hill came up with the idea of the postage stamp, Messrs Cooke and Wheatstone patented the first effective telegraph system, and Isambard Kingdom Brunel launched the SS *Great Western*.

While Bristol was celebrating the launch of the great steamship, which the next year opened the first regular transatlantic service powered by steam, a smaller port on the other side of the country, Great Yarmouth, was witnessing its own opening, if on a much smaller scale. And while the potential of the Great Western was obvious to most, few would have recognised that the opening of a small draper's shop, only 750 square feet in size, was just the start of an enterprise that could later claim to be the longest established department store in the country, a claim that has been successfully maintained in spite of the occasional challenge.

The draper's shop was opened by Garwood Burton Palmer, in the marketplace at Yarmouth. He was just twenty-two when he set his shop up; his unusual Christian names were the maiden names of both his mother and his grandmother. He was brought up in the nonconformist faith, having been christened in Middlegate Chapel on the 10 April 1815, just a couple of months before the Battle of Waterloo. Sadly the chapel was later destroyed by bombing in 1941.

The premises he chose had an interesting history, both as a granary store and as a pub, the 'Plow [sic] and Harrow'. The location could not have been bettered. Yarmouth was growing fast – its population doubled in the first half of the nineteenth century, and the Market Place was at its heart. Close by was the parish church, where a visiting preacher, the author's great grandfather, noted, in 1856, that the congregation numbered more than 3,000, including the mayor and council and the 'military in uniform, many of them wearing the Crimean medal, in the background the blue uniform of the artillery, contrasting picturesquely with the scarlet of the line'.

The Market Place may have been at the heart of the town, but it was also, literally, a bleeding heart. A visitor in the late eighteenth century described how butchers slaughtered calves and sheep in the Market Place, describing it as 'shocking to see in the centre of such an opulent town, resorted to by crowds of genteel company from almost every part of England'. This noxious nuisance continued unabated for another 100 years. Not enough, apparently, to put off Palmer's customers.

There was plenty to sustain the town's growth: trade with London, coal from the North East, and herrings for Italy and Spain were all facilitated by the splendid quay, described by Daniel Defoe in the late 1720s as the finest in Europe. Defoe described Yarmouth as being 'for wealth, trade and advantage of its situation, infinitely superior to Norwich'. Fish had been a major factor in the town's economy since Saxon times and became increasingly so. In the late eighteenth century Yarmouth had also been a whaling port – in 1764 seven Yarmouth ships returned from Greenland with seven whales. There was a flourishing coastal traffic, especially to Hull and Newcastle. That same visiting preacher, holidaying in the town in 1871, marvelled at the new fish wharf, recording that it was 780 feet long, under cover, and accommodating 'some hundreds of herring smacks from Holland, Scotland and France'. He went on to report that the 'catch was so prodigious that there is not enough salt for the fish, or casks in which to pack them'.

As transport improved, tourism developed fast. By the late nineteenth century the docks and jetties were welcoming trippers. For the August Bank Holiday of 1889 it was estimated that 2,000 arrived for the day in four steamers, augmenting the 2,600 who arrived by train on the same day. These trippers were following an eighteenth century influx of fashionable health tourists seeking benefit from the sea air, and the new arrivals didn't deter their wealthier counterparts. As late as 1862, a local diarist recorded the arrival in the town of a family friend arriving for his holiday with 'his family, four horses and three carriages'.

Garwood Palmer, founder of the store.

The interior of Palmer's original store.

Both the traditional fishing and the new tourism industries were augmented by the military presence in the town. The army and the navy each had a significant presence; major army barracks had been built there during the Napoleonic Wars, and Yarmouth's importance in naval terms was well established. It was to Gorleston that Nelson had returned after the Battle of the Nile, being taken by carriage to the Haven Bridge where cheering citizens replaced the horses and dragged him to the Wrestlers Inn. There he was to receive the Freedom of the Borough, but the clerk, having given him the Bible on which to swear, made an embarrassing faux pas. Nelson placed his left hand on the Bible to swear and the clerk told him it should be his right. 'That' said Nelson, 'is in Tenerife!' By Palmer's time though, the combination of army barracks and the naval hospital also created social advantages which enhanced the town's appeal to aspiring mothers like Mrs Bennett, whose main object in life was the appropriate marriage of daughters.

Obviously the growth of the town created strains. Perhaps it was the juxtaposition of the continental fishermen and the newly mobile trippers, but the incidence of arrests for drunkenness was six times as great in Yarmouth as in other resorts. Generally though crime was not a major issue; in 1891 the local paper rather endearingly reported that a boy had been summonsed for playing marbles on the pavement outside the town hall!

So Great Yarmouth was a thriving town – a perfect choice for a new retail enterprise. The Palmers had long been a leading local family with maritime connections, including shipbuilding. Garwood Palmer is remembered with a blue plaque on his former home in nearby Gorleston, an honour well merited by the continuing history of his enterprise, which celebrated its 175th year of trading in 2012. The house had an unusual history: it had been previously occupied by a succession of highly rated naval officers who made a habit of dying just at the point when it appeared they would achieve promotion to admiral. The house had been built originally by Capt. Cobb RN, who has the distinction of having been the only naval officer ever to be promoted to admiral after he had died. This bizarre occurrence arose because the board which made the appointment had not been apprised of his death when they met.

Palmer had trained in London with a prominent city firm of drapers, Hitchcock & Rogers, then of Ludgate Hill. He may just have been a contemporary there of Sir George Williams, who later became, having married Hitchcock's daughter, a partner in the renamed firm of Hitchcock & Williams, which moved to St Paul's churchyard, and its sole proprietor on Hitchcock's death. Both partners were of a charitable disposition and Williams is perhaps best known as the founder of the YMCA, whose first meeting, in 1844, took place on the firm's premises. The firm shared with Palmer's a succession of generations involved in its management. Sadly it did not share Palmer's longevity. Hitchcock & Williams closed in 1984, with one of the fifth generation of Williams' family members on the board right until to the end.

Garwood Palmer's training in London obviously stood him in good stead, for the business prospered from the beginning and he soon became a familiar sight driving his carriage from his home in Gorleston to the store, perhaps being especially careful on the Southtown Rd, which was the scene of an accident that killed another family member, who was thrown out of his carriage there in 1850. Garwood Palmer was a man of some style, decorating his store with flowers and ferns from his own garden, and presenting shoppers with complimentary nosegays on occasion. And it seems he didn't restrict himself just to retailing, the 1861 census lists his occupation as 'Ship Owner', following in his family tradition.

In 1844 he took his younger brother Nathaniel into partnership, and when Nathaniel died, in 1862 at the age of just thirty-eight, Garwood, who had no children of his own, continued to run the business until the 1870s, when he was joined by Nathaniel's sons, Ernest Edward and James Hurry, thus ensuring the continuation of the family's management of the store. With their help the store continued to thrive, and by the 1880s had a depth of 200 feet despite its narrow frontage.

At that time it was usual for many of the staff at larger stores to live in. Palmer's was no different in this respect, but is unusual in that there remains sufficient evidence to paint a fairly detailed picture of how such arrangements worked, and what it must have been like to be one of the resident staff. The housekeeper was given very full instructions on how to perform her role and the rules she was to impose. This book, dating from around 1884, gives a wonderfully complete picture of life for the staff.

Both men and women were accommodated but strictly segregated: 'Young men are not allowed in the young ladies sitting room' was a natural restriction, but why 'Young ladies sleeping out are to use the lavatory in the ante-room' was another rule is more difficult to comprehend.

There were formalities to be observed. Rather like a colonial mess or a formal dinner party, the position in which one sat at table was a matter of precedence, and in this case,

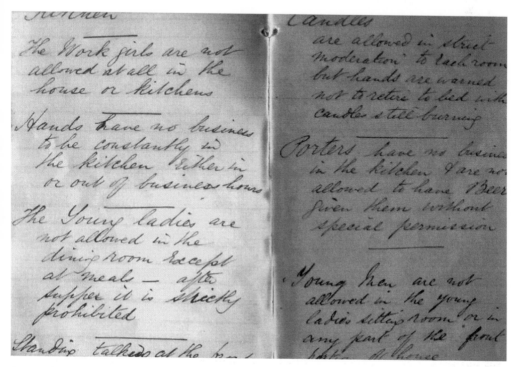

A page from the *Housekeeper's Book of Rules*.

of gender too. 'The hands all sit in seniority at the table, and are served in that order each meal, ladies first, gentlemen next.' If you were young, male, and very junior your food was probably cold when you got it. Punctuality was expected, faddiness deplored. 'Assistants being late, or refusing to keep the rules are to be reported to Mr Hurry (Palmer). Assistants who continually grumble at the food provided are to be reported'. Good manners were expected 'reading at meals is prohibited, except at tea'. To enforce all this, the housekeeper was 'to preside' at breakfast, tea and supper, while for dinner 'one member of the firm will carve at one end, the housekeeper presiding at the other'.

The food, about which they were not to complain, was plain, solid fare served in a formulaic procession reminiscent of school meals in the 1950s, when there was no need for a diary because one always knew the day from the food. Beef, preceded by 'light dumplings and gravey' [sic] was served twice weekly. Yorkshire pudding or boiled batter with 'gravey and hot meat' once. Except in summer, another standard was either fish or soup, with no pudding. On the other two days of the six-day working week there was 'some kind of pudding or pies with hot or cold meat'. For breakfast there was tea, bread and butter (cut thin for the girls and thicker for the boys) but on Sundays there was also ham or cold boiled bacon. If the former then only half a ham was to be provided, the other half being reserved for the following weekend. Thin bread for the girls and thicker for the boys was provided for tea too, except on Tuesdays and Thursdays when, if there was enough dripping available, shortcakes with currants would be provided too. On Sundays, 'if convenient', there might be a 'little home-made plum cake'. But this extravagance was at a cost – Sunday supper was to comprise 'Bread, cheese and butter only'.

There were exceptions, of course. On Good Friday members of staff were allowed one egg each, and a Hot Cross Bun, while at Christmas there was fowl, plum pudding and 'a dessert arranged by Mr Hurry'.

The provision of food was governed by clearly laid down stipulations as to what was to be spent. Economy was expected, and under-linings emphasised the point. For example, Thursday supper was to be served at 9.30 p.m. and the instructions were 'On this night they occasionally finish up odd pieces but it is not to be made a rule as nothing is to be bought in specially for this meal & if any complaint is made, allow only the ordinary plain supper without any exception whatever.'

The grocer's list was in the hands of Mr Hurry, though butter could be bought on the market once a week, but only if the cost was less than one shilling and sixpence per lb. If not available at that price then unsalted 'Brittany Butter' was to be purchased at one shilling and fourpence. The negotiations were to be carried out by Mr Hurry, who was also responsible for deciding on the quantity of bread needed, and for checking the prices paid for just about everything else. Bizarrely, while all other vegetables were not charged for by the company, potatoes were. The explanation may be that the other vegetables and fruit came from the Palmers' garden at Gorleston. As for meat, Mr Hurry was to be consulted on where to order it, but the types were laid down in the rules: 'have mutton once or twice a week, legs principally, but sometimes shoulders. Beef - the Crown Piece or Half Leg or, for Sundays, Ribs'. This latter seems at odds with another rule 'Dinners on Sundays. Cold meat. Celery, lettuces or pickle. Cold pies or tarts. No cooking allowed at all.'

Other parameters were clearly drawn too. 'Beer. The key to be kept by housekeeper, or by cook if to be trusted. The consumption is to be carefully watched to see that an unlimited quantity is not allowed. Two glasses allowed to each young lady and two to each young man.' Drinking was to be discouraged by the housekeeper and 'any secret drinking was to be reported'. As for milk, one glass was to be allowed at supper 'if have enough in the house'.

In the evenings the front door was latched at 10.00 p.m., by which time all apprentices and staff under the age of twenty-one had to be in, and finally locked at 10.30 p.m. by when all other assistants had to have returned. All staff had to retire to bed at 10.45 p.m. Permission was 'occasionally' given by Mr Hurry or Mr Ernest (the Palmer brothers) to stay out until 11.00 p.m., 'but never for a later hour'.

To light their evenings candles were allowed 'in strict moderation' but to be extinguished before retiring to bed. 'Reading in bed by candle is strictly prohibited'. Fire was obviously a constant threat, perhaps recognised even more after fire gutted the store in 1892. 'When the alarm bell in the ante-room rings, all hands are at once to come into the shop'. The fire on 29 November 1892, of which more later, made national news, the *Morning Post* reporting that 'some of the assistants had narrow escapes, and many of them lost their clothes, money and other valuables'. The damage to the premises was estimated at several thousand pounds, but the report added, reassuringly, that the property was insured!

Female emancipation was a long way in the future: 'the young ladies all make their own beds, but the young men's beds require making' ran one instruction and 'every room is to be dusted every morning and properly cleaned every week. All mattresses are to be brushed once a month when clean sheets are put on'. Perhaps to ensure no contact between the young men and the maids who made their beds there was another rule: 'The young men are not allowed to go to their rooms after 9 o'clock until after the shop closes. They must bring down what things they require when they leave in the morning. This is to be strictly enforced.'

Illness was frowned upon: 'only in very urgent cases is brandy or other spirit to be supplied'. Illness was the only occasion on which food could be taken to the rooms, and even then required the permission of the housekeeper. Cleanliness was not comfortably maintained, hot water was supplied only 'occasionally, the same if baths are required'.

A page in the rule book sets out clearly the approach of the partners: 'The desire of the firm is that the assistants should be made comfortable & the strict enforcement of these rules will be most likely to conduce to that end; the interests of the firm being always carefully studied & protected.' Probably the assistants were content to put up with the various limitations on their freedom. They were living in a secure environment, getting regular meals and being looked after by team of domestic staff.

Much must have depended on the attitude of the housekeeper, but her manner probably had even more impact on the domestic staff. Familiarity was not encouraged; she was instructed to show no favouritism and to 'be kind but firm'. She was to visit the kitchen several times a day 'to see what is going on there and prevent noise or too much play'. 'Followers' were clearly not encouraged 'standing talking at the door is not allowed', 'hands have no business to be constantly in the kitchen', and 'hangers on at the back doors not allowed'. The servants themselves had a hard life. They were expected to be up at

6.30 a.m. and their duties were clearly defined – the book even lists who is to clean which rooms. The maids had not only to clean the rooms, but serve at meal times. The cook was allowed to go out two evenings a week, and the maids one and a half! Their wages were regulated, the cook earning between £14 and £18 a year and the maids between £10 and £14. 'If tired' they were allowed to retire at 10.00 p.m. on alternate weeks, and the housemaid 'who sleeps in the little room' was charged with turning off the gas tap at 10.45 p.m. They were allowed one week's holiday a year. Not much of a life, but then domestic service was hard anywhere and at least they were safe, warm and fed.

The tradition of staff living on the premises continued for many years. In 1907, as many as seventy staff, around 35 per cent of the total, were still accommodated, although by now the sexes had been segregated with the men living in a house nearby while the women still lived over the shop; as late as 1941, when the store suffered bomb damage, some staff were still living on the premises.

Garwood Palmer died in 1888, but the business continued to prosper under the control of his two nephews, and became known as 'Palmer Bros.'. One of the first crises with which they had to cope was that fire in 1892. It started in the early hours of Wednesday 29 November, and engulfed most of the rear part of three of the four linked shops which comprised the retail premises and workshops. The alarm was raised by Mrs Jennings, the head dressmaker who, with a number of assistants, lived over one of the shops. She told the local press that she had been awakened by the 'sweet music' of the Christmas waifs outside. At three o'clock in the morning and nearly a month before Christmas, one can only wonder just how 'sweet' the music was. It was loud enough, anyway, to wake her and she could smell smoke coming from below. Rapidly dressing, she alerted the other residents, some of whom had to escape in their nightdresses.

The arrangements for dealing with fires were unsophisticated. Alerted by shouts from the window, a patrolling constable ran to the police station and the Water Works Co. was informed. It took half an hour for the first engine to arrive; local residents helped to lay out the hoses but the stream of water from the small manual engine was woefully inadequate, and the fire spread rapidly. It was another hour and a half before a second engine arrived, and that was no more effective. The speed of the fire was probably accelerated by the inflammable nature of some of the stock, such as the muslin and ribbons. By five o'clock the roof of one department had fallen in, and others followed. No long ladders were available so hoses could only be played from ground level, and the fire raged on. It took until half-past seven for it to be mainly extinguished, by which time, said the press report, 'the wreckage was complete' and the policemen who had helped to fight the fire were looking 'more like chimney-sweeps than guardians of the law'. The stock was almost completely destroyed and of the buildings, only the façade and, fortunately, the southernmost shop remained undamaged. This last was something of a blessing, enabling Palmers to continue to trade from at least part of the premises. Among the wreckage of broken Oriental ware and pottery, fancy articles and general debris was found a cash box with £12 in gold, belonging to one of the assistants, and a bent and battered bedstead which had fallen through when the upper floor collapsed. Mr Hurry was quoted as saying that the store might have been saved if there had been adequate provision of fire engines – certainly the delays and lack of equipment didn't help.

After the fire of 1892.

Following the fire some staff were accommodated in a local hotel; others were put up by some of the Palmers' friends and, remarkably, others by customers – a tribute to the success of the emphasis the firm had always laid on developing close relationships with them. Helped by the ability to continue trading, albeit on a smaller scale, from the remaining premises and by the settling of the insurance claim, Palmer Brothers, as the firm was then styled, made an impressive recovery and was soon growing faster than ever. The energy of the two brothers, the bustling Mr Hurry and the quieter Mr Ernest, was matched by their acumen and new lines were added in a welter of expansion. At the turn of the century, *Kelly's Directory* listed Palmers as 'family drapers and silk mercers, hosiers, lacemen, dress and mantle makers, millinery and fancy goods importers, carpet warehousemen and complete house furnishers' and gave their premises as Nos 37, 38, 38A, and 39 Market place. In some ways the fire had been a boon for Palmer's. In much the same way that Germany gained an economic advantage after the Second World War by having to build afresh using the most modern techniques and plant to restart its industries, so Palmers were able to rebuild taking advantage of many of the developments of the Victorian era.

By 1907, when the firm celebrated its seventieth anniversary, the store could boast thirty-one departments and a floor area more than thirty times the size of the original premises. An air of spaciousness is evident in photographs of the period. There were elegant showrooms for such items as millinery, busy and crowded departments for small items such as ribbons and laces, and large displays of carpets, curtains and furnishings. The furniture showrooms were necessarily large and crowded, but still gave an air of spaciousness with the subtle use of natural light from skylights. Everywhere chairs were

The 'Fancy Bazaar', Palmer's.

Millinery Department, Palmer's.

provided for the comfort of customers while they were offered a wide range of goods. The comfort of customers was further enhanced by luxurious fitting rooms adjacent to the workshop where the dressmakers plied their craft. One can picture ladies, waiting for alterations and between fittings, spending the odd hour pleasurably in the Jewellery department while their children coveted the toys in the adjoining Fancy Bazaar.

The comfort of the staff was considered too. There was an elegant staff dining room of impressive proportions – 1,200 square feet with bay windows overlooking the market place. Palmers, the firm had reverted to this style a few years earlier, was proud of its modern approach. Two telephone were lines were installed, the numbers 566 and 567 and the means was available to connect callers to all departments. Communication between these departments was by speaking tubes. The store was the first public building in Yarmouth to be lit by electricity, in 1902.

Palmer's pride and joy was their Pneumatic Tube Cash system, which, it was claimed, enabled customers in those pre-credit card days to get their change much quicker. The brochure produced by Palmers to celebrate the seventieth anniversary described the mechanism, worked by a patent suction engine and an electric motor:

The cash is inserted in metal carriers, which in turn are put into a brass tube, thorough which air is being circulated at high pressure. Six seconds is sufficient for the carrier to reach the first floor desk from the longest outstation, 250 feet away. The change is then returned by the cashier in another tube, and arrives back, often within twenty seconds of being despatched.

Palmer's cashier.

Similar equipment, little changed, was still being used in some shops as late as the end of the 1940s and early 1950s. The brochure also pictures the cashier on the first floor, sitting at a desk dominated by a pair of upright tubes resembling trombones for the use of giants. She sits calmly, arms folded and hands resting on her lap, waiting for a sale to be registered. How she was able, at busy times, to open arriving tubes, check the bill of sale, put the money safely away, count the change, put it in the tube and send it in the eight seconds which would be available to her to meet the twenty-second target is a mystery. There appears to have been just one operative and one set of tubes to receive and despatch the carriers. At busy times, and in Sales, the collection of carriers must have resembled the M25 at rush hour – perhaps the chairs provided for customers earned their keep at such times!

Stocktaking in those days was a major event and had some resonance with harvest time in the countryside, especially as it finished, when there was a Stocktaking Supper, usually in mid-March, which was under the control of Mr Hurry Palmer. The scale of the enterprise was substantial. A cold joint of beef was provided with two rabbit pies, and two pork pies. Eight-dozen 'Fancy Tarts', thirty custards, and fifty jellies were provided with fifty small loaves of bread, fifty oranges, 6 lbs of apples and 3 lbs of figs. All this was washed down with four dozen of lemonade, one dozen of ginger beers and one of ginger ale. Ironically for a store with a huge china and glass department, all the crockery was hired. If the table in the staff dining room was not large enough then the supper was to be held in the carpet department, for which eight trestle tables and one side table were borrowed from a school.

Replete with all these goodies the staff were then offered 'amusements' of a type unspecified in one of the workshops, but only until the iron tongue of midnight had struck when presumably the resident staff at least could retire upstairs to their accommodation.

It was in the 1900s that Palmers again showed their commitment both to staff and to the expansion of the company by introducing an apprentice scheme. The premium they charged the parents of such apprentices was £20 (around £1,800 today, having regard to inflation), a lot for many parents to find but only half what competitors such as Jarrold's had been charging for many years. And they were still charging only the same as late as 1937. The indenture, as with that of Jarrold's, did require the parent or guardian to provide for the apprentice, this time in respect of clothing, medical costs and 'other necessaries', but Jarrold's clauses banning marriage, fornication and gambling were missing.

In 1908 James Hurry Palmer had died, and his son Percy Hurry Palmer joined the business in partnership with his uncle Ernest. Percy was to influence enormously the future shape of Palmers, not least as the man responsible in the 1930s for the incorporation of the business as a limited company, instead of its traditional partnership arrangements.

The store continued to grow. In 1910 the premises were extensively enlarged and in 1912 new furnishing workshops were opened, but the First World War checked progress for a while. Great Yarmouth suffered both shelling from the Kaiser's Grand Fleet and bombing from a German Navy Zeppelin which had been prevented from attacking its initial targets in Humberside by bad weather. Conscription led to staff shortages in the area, and these were matched by shortages of basic foodstuffs – even the racecourse was turned into a giant vegetable patch. It was not an easy time for civilians or for retailers, but Palmers emerged relatively unscathed. After the war there came first the 'roaring twenties' followed of course by the Great Depression. Again Palmer's showed its mettle.

One delightful incident in the 1920s bears mention. Percy Palmer was a patron of the Norfolk and Norwich Triennial Arts Festival, in which capacity he happened to meet Sir Henry Wood, best known for the Proms named after him. The story goes that he had broken his conductor's baton, and Palmer offered to make a replacement for him in Palmers workshops. Clearly Sir Henry was pleased with the result because he commissioned batons regularly from Palmers for the remaining twenty years or so of his life. In his book *About Conducting*, Sir Henry confirms this story:

> I have had my batons made for many years by a firm in Great Yarmouth, Palmer's. It came about that one of those interested in the firm, a diligent follower of all the fine Norwich festivals of those days, asked permission to make them for me, and so they have ever since.

Sir Henry was a demanding patron; his specifications for the batons were most precise and various weights, woods and balance points were required at different times. The first baton, dating from around 1921, is preserved at Palmers store to this day.

Sir Henry Wood with conducting batons made by Palmer's.

Palmer's Store, 1937.

The 1930s was the decade in which the company was incorporated as a limited company, and, of course, of its centenary celebrations. The partnership was beginning to become unwieldy as family members died, leaving their share of the partnership across a number of heirs who were not directly involved in running the business. Percy decided to tidy things up. He wanted a situation in which he could determine both the strategy of the business and its tactics without having to gain the approval of a host of relatives, some holding only a small share of the partnership and having too little practical involvement with the business to be able to contribute constructively to its policy. The means upon which he hit was to incorporate but to buy out the partners in Preference Shares – a class of share which gave the holder first call on dividends and offered some protection in the event of insolvency but which, importantly, carried no voting rights. By himself holding most of the Ordinary Shares, which did carry voting rights, he was able to control the destiny of the company with less interference. It was a 'cunning plan' which even Baldrick might have admired. The attraction to the other partners of the knowledge that they had a right to dividends which took precedence over that of Percy, and the assurance that they would have first call on the assets in the event of bankruptcy, proved attractive enough for them to forgo their voting rights. It was an effective ploy.

The centenary itself was celebrated in a very practical way, with the production of a ceremonial blotter book, the pages of blotting paper being interspersed with illustrations of the store and text about its history. Bruce Sturrock, grandson of Percy and the present chairman of Palmers relates the story of Percy's disappointment with one aspect of this novel memorial to the first 100 years. Apparently Percy was a man who took the greatest care with all he wrote and placed great emphasis on correct spelling and grammar. The opening page of the blotter book comprised a printed version of a handwritten Introduction from Percy; he was mortified, after the books were printed, to notice that he had misspelled the word 'memento' by inserting an 'o' in the place of the first 'e'. The store itself had become a picture of elegance, and the blotter book both celebrated this and drew attention to its long history in the world of fashion.

The story told in the blotter book was one of continuing success, of expansion, of modernisation and improvement – the company faced the future with confidence. But war was just around the corner, with its shortages of stock and of men, and with Yarmouth effectively in the front line on the home front because of its naval base, the risk of bombs too. Added to the deliberate bombing of the town was the risk of German bombers returning home having not located their intended targets simply jettisoning their load as they crossed the coast.

Great Yarmouth suffered grievously in the war, and Palmer's was not exempt. In a sad letter sent by Percy after a raid to a non-executive director on 8 April 1941 he wrote,

we thought we had saved the men's shop block entirely. Kath (his wife) and I went up to the end of King Street to see if one of our furniture depositories was safe. We had barely got there when a land mine came down and exploded within 50/60 yards of us. We returned to find that the fire from next door, which we thought out, had spread to the flat above the display workshop. As they were flooding it with water we had to stay and clear the whole stock from the men's shop. This is the third try within a week that they have had to burn down Yarmouth,

April 1937   Sharlet Place
                Gt Yarmouth

Dear Sir or Madam.

    May I ask your acceptance of this blotter and its story of my firm's progress since 1837 as a memento of our Centenary.

    I am very proud that my association with the House of Palmers covers a third of its history, and look back with deep appreciation of the support accorded me by customers of the firm throughout that time. Without that support such success as I have achieved would have been impossible.

    Although times have changed and loyalties are less binding I still like to think our customers are in a sense friends of the firm.

    In these days of standardisation I am anxious to preserve that personal element which makes for confidence between customer and supplier, and it is through this ideal of personal service by principals and staff that I hope to merit your confidence in the future.

        Faithfully yours

Palmer's Centenary Blotter – complete with spelling mistake.

An artist's impression of the Main Shop after 1937 alterations

Interior of Palmer's Men's Shop, 1937.

but the other two missed by a mile or more'. With obvious and justified pride he added 'Our staff on duty or living over the premises behaved magnificently, and saving the main premises is due to them.'

In that year over 100 civilians died as a result of the raids, and on that occasion alone it was estimated that 4,000 incendiary bombs fell on the town. In June the following year the great church of St Nicholas, where my great-grandfather had, on several occasions, preached to congregations of three or even 4,000, the biggest parish church in the country, was totally destroyed by bombs. It took until 1961 for the church to be rebuilt and reconsecrated.

During the war, with its hardships and very limited availability of stock, Percy Palmer had acted with commendable presence of mind. Realising that a lot of properties had been damaged to an extent which made them uninhabitable he decided to put his stock-starved premises to good use, turning them into storage depositories for furniture from bomb damaged homes – a source of reassurance to the home owner, and income to the store.

The war and its aftermath was a difficult period; the national shortages and rationing were exacerbated in Yarmouth both by the slow rate of restoration of bomb damage and changing local conditions. The two traditional staple industries were both changing. From being a place at which the wealthy took the sea air, Yarmouth had become a resort targeting a different market, larger but with less to spend, and such spending was often within the confines of the holiday camps and parks which sprang up almost overnight like mushrooms.

More noticeable still was the decline of the herring industry. Already shrinking before the war, as few new boats joined a diminishing fleet which had in the early years of the twentieth century, comprised around 1,000 boats; the trend accelerated after the war and twenty-five years later the catch of herring was just one hundredth of 1 per cent of the catch in 1913. The traditional source of Yarmouth's prosperity had simply been airbrushed out.

Percy Palmer did not have to cope with these issues alone. In 1947 his son-in-law Graham Sturrock joined the firm as a trainee, taking over as managing director seven years later; Percy remained chairman until his death in 1960. Graham Sturrock was a man who recognised that in a changing world an independent store would only survive if it changed too. Writing at the time of the 125th anniversary of the store in 1962, he regretted the loss of independence experienced by many similar stores, but maintained that there was, and would remain, a place for them in the future. To ensure this he believed that the trick was to expand, while retaining the old core values which had made the store successful in the past. Given the changing economic conditions of Yarmouth, and the firm's already dominant position in the town he made a strategic decision to expand by acquisitions elsewhere. His plan was to take over smaller independent stores in towns in East Anglia, bringing them into the Palmer fold and gaining economies of scale by centralising the key functions of management, such as buying and pricing.

His early acquisitions were in Lowestoft, Bury St Edmunds, Spalding and Holbeach. All except the Bury St Edmunds acquisition were specialist menswear shops, and his intention was to develop a chain of such shops to operate in parallel with the department stores. Part of the rationale behind this was that his merchandise director 'Shep' Shepherd had a particular expertise in this field. His plans changed with the untimely death of Mr Shepherd and after a few years these were disposed of. Bury was a different matter, proving a great success and leading to later expansion in that town; much later there was also to be a much more substantial acquisition in Lowestoft, led by his son, Bruce Sturrock, during a later period of expansion. Often the targets comprised old established independent stores which were finding the rapidly changing marketplace difficult. Although each of the acquisitions was in East Anglia, geographic proximity was not the driving factor in their choice – although Lowestoft was a near neighbour and another former fishing port and fashionable resort, the others were not. The towns of Holbeach and Spalding were at quite a distance but the stores he bought there were specialist menswear outlets and their acquisition helped to broaden the overall product range. Bury had no obvious link to any of the others but the store was successful and offered the possibility of creating a wider geographical spread. What sometimes attracted Sturrock was the ability to integrate the management of the stores within Palmers' own system, the fact that each had a history of sharing the values in customer relations which had served Palmers so well, and that they all enjoyed a good name in their own area. This last enabled him to differentiate his acquisition policy from that of the major store groups. In their case it was pretty well standard procedure to rebrand the new outlets to mirror that of the new owners. After all, the cost of promoting their brand demanded that it was used to the best advantage. Sturrock followed a different route, deciding to allow the acquired stores to continue to trade under their traditional titles, thus giving a degree of reassurance to local residents that the traditional values remained intact. It was a policy which made sense: to leverage the existing reputation and avoid the cost of promoting the Palmer brand in areas where it was not well known.

Another policy to address the new challenges was to extend the already wide range of services the store could provide, and by the 1960s the customer could book a holiday, hire a morning suit for a family wedding, have Christmas cards and stationery printed, arrange costumes for the cast at local theatres, have furniture made to his own specification or even arrange for his household goods to be removed to a new address anywhere in the country. Palmers was finding ways to deal with a changing local economy, and in 1971 Graham Sturrock was joined by his son Bruce, who, having trained with another independent store, became manager of the store at Bury St Edmunds where he held sway for six years before joining his father at Yarmouth, succeeding him as managing director in 1983, at which point his father became chairman.

Bruce Sturrock's arrival at the flagship store had been a significant moment for the company. He had been very successful in generating profit in the store in Bury and was well equipped to plot a course through the immensely challenging retail scene. Social changes, which brought almost universal access to a car, and improved communication networks, meant that the competition was no longer restricted to Yarmouth. Increasingly the nationals were expanding and many had arrived in Norwich which was easily accessed by traditional Palmer's customers. Further, the development of out of town shopping centres, also made possible by the universality of the car, added a new ingredient to the retail pot. It is not much of an exaggeration to suggest that these developments were, in their way, almost as big a threat to the traditional store as the internet is today. In a town no longer as fashionable as it once was, and with clear signs of economic decay, Palmer's traditional emphasis on value and exceptional service was no longer enough.

There was still, though, time to mark the store's 150th anniversary, which was celebrated in style with a visit from HRH Princess Alexandra on 4 June 1987. Huge crowds defied the summer rain to catch a glimpse of her after she had toured the store and met many of the staff. Before she left she was presented with a bouquet by Bruce's daughter Emma, then aged three, and now, in 2015, an executive director of the firm. Palmers enjoyed the day and marked the anniversary with a range of commemorative products, decorated mugs, plates and paperweights.

Celebrations aside, something had to be done to meet the new environment and Bruce Sturrock proved to be his father's son. H
e determined that the answer was expansion beyond the confines of Yarmouth and embarked on a new programme of acquisition, believing that his management team had the capacity to handle additional outlets. In 1990 he bought the former Bonds store in Dereham and two years later added Ashfords, a department store in Newmarket. In 1998 he acquired further premises in Bury, enabling the company to operate distinctively as a fashion store in one location and to focus on linens and

homeware in the other. A further acquisition in Kings Lynn was followed, in 2004, by the biggest coup of them all – the purchase of Chadds, an old established department store in Lowestoft which on its own added 25,000 square feet of shop floor. In the fifteen years to 2004, the business grew to have seven branches, manned by 450 staff, and a turnover in excess of £20 million. Helping him in this was his sister Wendy Cole, back from Bloomingdale's in New York where she had been fashion buyer, who in 1993 entered the fray full of ideas and enthusiasm. She joined as fashion director.

Bruce Sturrock had inherited a situation which would have been familiar to his grandfather, whose efforts to rationalise the partnership by incorporating and holding all the voting shares himself had enabled him successfully to build the business. Half a century later the problems Percy had solved started to recur. Percy's own shares had been bequeathed by him to a number of family members and, with each new generation, the number of small shareholders grew to include many with less active involvement in the business.

At a time when significant new challenges needed to be faced up to, Bruce Sturrock decided that he must, as his grandfather had before, restructure the company to secure its future. He had tried to reach an agreement at the time he started the company's growth strategy, but the family were not ready. However following lengthy family discussions, twenty shareholders accepted an offer for their shares and, in 2005, Bruce and his sister Wendy became the joint owners of the company. It is something of an irony that in order to raise the capital to buy out the existing shareholders, the policy of expansion had to be reversed and the stores in Newmarket and King's Lynn were sold.

Palmer's continued to thrive and in February 2012 celebrated its 175th anniversary with another royal visit, this time by HRH the Prince of Wales. Twenty-five years on it was again Emma Sturrock making a presentation, this time of a celebratory cake. The Prince toured the store with Bruce and Wendy, and took a knife to the cake Emma had presented, watched over by Bruce Sturrock, to the evident amusement of them both.

At around the same time there were changes in the management structure of the company. Emma Sturrock had been working in an internet business for some time, and joined the company to set up its own online business extending the number of generations of the family involved in running the business to six, and she joined the Board in 2015. Again in 2012 Bruce Sturrock decided to devote his energies to ensuring that Palmers continued to operate strategically in a way that matched a rapidly changing retail environment and moved to the role of chairman. The company appointed to the board its first non-family member, David Howard, an experienced retailer, as managing director to look after the day to day running of the business.

There is a comfortable feeling when one enters the store with its traditional appearance, and the breadth of the range of products. These days many lines are handled by the suppliers themselves, who take the responsibility for managing some space and provide and train their own staff. Bruce Sturrock describes how over the years he has turned Palmers from a department store into 'a store with departments'. That may seem a fine distinction but it is an important one. A department store is one, he says, that has effectually to have departments which offer just about everything. His achievement has been to create a much greater degree of flexibility by being willing to try new lines and dispose of old

Emma Sturrock presenting a cake to HRH the Prince of Wales.

The Prince of Wales enjoying a joke with Bruce Sturrock.

ones when change demands. And such changes can arise not just from changing fashion but from a changing trading environment. It is that flexibility which has enabled Palmers to survive in an era when all retailers have struggled with a public unwilling or unable to spend as before and when the advance of, first, out of town shopping centres and, more recently, the internet has been such a challenge. There are always new challenges to meet and good strategic planning will be essential to secure the future.

One thing that seems unlikely to change is the value that the company puts on customer relationships; walking through the store with Bruce Sturrock the importance attached to these by the customers themselves is evident. He is greeted by name by many of them, and it is clear the interest, even affection, is reciprocated. Whatever the future holds that special brand of service seems certain to remain a key feature of this store.

W. J. Aldiss of Fakenham –
'The People's Draper'

Family tree of those members of the Aldiss family mentioned in this chapter.

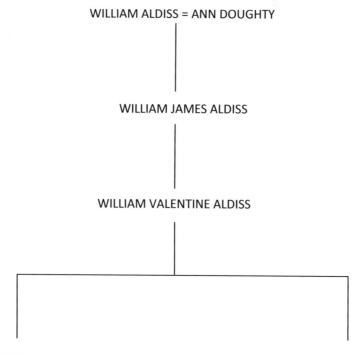

WILLIAM ALDISS = ANN DOUGHTY

WILLIAM JAMES ALDISS

WILLIAM VALENTINE ALDISS

WILLIAM JAMES ALDISS

TIMOTHY CHRISTOPHER ALDISS

Fakenham Market Place *c.* 1920 – 'The People's Draper'.

Fakenham jubilee celebrations, 1887.

Fakenham in the 1890s was a major centre of printing, with nearly 10 per cent of the town's population working in the industry, but it was also still an important market town with biannual cattle fairs and an annual sheep fair. The town celebrated Victoria's Diamond Jubilee in style. The town benefited from a wide range of shops, providing for the needs of those coming in from the outlying farms on market day as well as those working in the town. There had been at least one bank in the town since the late eighteenth century and the housing stock was relatively modern. As one would expect in those less secular days, even with a population of only around 2,000 there were plenty of places of worship. Non-conformism was a major force, and the parish church of St Peter and St Paul, restored in the mid-nineteenth century, jockeyed for position with the meeting places of Plymouth Brethren, Primitive Methodists, Salvationists, Wesleyans, Baptists and, from the early twentieth century, Roman Catholics. Communications had always been quite good. Even in the days of coaches Fakenham was a stop on the way from Burnham Market to London, a perhaps surprising route so long before the advent of the London weekender! Later the coach connected with the London-bound train at Brandon, but by 1880 Fakenham could boast two separate railway stations of its own, the Lynn and Fakenham Railway having opened a new station at Hempton, confusingly called Fakenham West, in 1880; a fragment of the platform still survives though the line was closed in 1959. Overall it was a prosperous, well-ordered (it had its own magistrates' court) and forward-looking community – by 1890 it already had a 'Motor Garage'. With the added attraction for a retailer of regular visitors on market days, it was a good choice of town in which to open a draper's business.

It was in 1892 that William James Aldiss opened his first shop – a drapery, at Norwich Road, Fakenham. The capital to enable him to do so was lent by his widowed mother, Ann Doughty Aldiss. Clearly she was a lady anxious to see her sons settled in business because she also advanced money to William's brother, Harry Hildyard Aldiss, to open a similar shop in Dereham. William appears to have been her favourite though – Harry's loan was at 4 per cent interest; William's was interest free. Ann was a woman of means. At her death in 1902 her estate included no less than eleven loans and mortgages, often on the security of draper's shops, as well as high-yielding overseas bonds issued in the Argentine and Canadian shares in a number of British companies. From whence she derived her capital originally is unclear, but she must either have been unusually well informed about financial matters for a lady in the late nineteenth century, or perhaps in receipt of expert advice. Her late husband, William Aldiss, a draper himself, in Swaffham, had died in 1873. He had made provision for Ann during her life and the balance of his estate was shared equally between the two brothers and their surviving sister, Emily, their three siblings having died in infancy. William Senior would seem to have been in a substantial way of business – by the time of distribution (on Ann's death) in 1903 the value of the remaining assets in his estate was around £4,700 – well over £400,000 in today's values. His assets might have been greater; the estate account in 1902 shows a small final dividend in respect of the bankruptcy of Harvey & Hudson's Bank. Actually, by the time of its insolvency the bank was called Crown Bank and was owned by Sir Robert Harvey MP, who brought about the failure by fraudulently removing funds with which to further his political career and to speculate on the stock market. This final dividend was paid, it appears, as long as thirty-three years after the failure. Ann's own assets were even more substantial.

The loan to William, of £150, together with a loan from his father's estate, of £350 (today around £50,000) was still outstanding at her death in 1902, but William had made good use of it and his business was thriving. At his own death, in 1933, the probate valuation of his estate was almost £70,000, equivalent to approximately £4.3 million in 2014. In 1928 in his Deed Box at the bank were deposited the deeds of thirty-six properties, both residential and commercial. He seems to have been a bit coy about this; the receipt from the Bank simply refers to 'a large black tin box, locked, contents unknown'. Perhaps he preferred to keep the bank in the dark, or perhaps the bank was merely exercising its customary caution. He was also an active trader in Gilts – one of the few to make a profit on War Loan. He examined his bank statements closely. In 1933 he spotted an erroneous debit of £127.16.10d which was promptly rectified by the bank – the confirming credit is still attached to the compliment slip, the bank official has simply added the words 'and regrets' to the printed 'With the Manager's Compliments', perhaps a rather inadequate apology to an excellent customer. And he was an excellent customer. In 1927 he made an offer to buy the bank's own premises, and in October of that year the manager wrote to Aldiss telling him that the local board of the bank was recommending their head office to accept his offer. They instructed the branch manager to 'explain to Mr Aldiss that we very much prefer credit accounts to overdrawn ones and we quite appreciate the good accounts that have been kept with us. We are most anxious to oblige him, and are glad that he has made an offer that we can recommend'.

The original store had soon proved inadequate and William opened new premises. He was an expansionist by nature, as was his son William Valentine Aldiss ('Mr Val') who developed an institution called 'The Club', which was promoted by the roundsmen who delivered locally. Effectually Aldiss acted as a Banker. Small amounts were collected by the roundsmen and held by the store against future purchases, rather like the 'Christmas Clubs' of more recent times. Then as now the benefit to the store is that the money is payment for the deferred supply of goods. But with Aldiss, there was a twist: customers using their accumulated funds were entitled to a 10 per cent discount on goods bought in the store. This incentive was funded both by the inherent profit in the later sale and by the ability to use the cash in the interim. The store was happy, the money could only be spent on goods purchased from it, and the customer was also happy, getting a significant return on his savings with no tax to pay. In fact so successful was the scheme that it continued for nearly thirty years after William died; its death knell only sounded in the middle of the twentieth-century arrival of the 'Live Now, Pay Later' generation for whom Hire Purchase meant not having to wait for anything, and the more universal development of price discounting.

Fine new premises had been acquired in 1907 in the Market Place, and the company traded under the slogan of 'The People's Draper'; its advertisements just a year later proclaimed them to be 'The People's Popular Draper, Outfitter and Boot Merchant'. In 1931 these premises were significantly improved and William modelled his plans with a view to replicating as far as possible the style and appearance of Swan & Edgar in Piccadilly. By now the firm had slightly changed its slogan, and anyone telephoning

Aldiss shop front, 1930s.

Fakenham 28 would have found themselves connected to 'The People's Draper and Milliner'.

The slogan 'The People's Draper' is somewhat at odds with the customers William Aldiss had known in his days as an apprentice as seen in the invoice book he had kept at that time – professional men and titled ladies are much in evidence. The nature of contemporary fashions was perhaps responsible for one such lady buying enough silk in one day to cover a cricket pitch, enough satin and velvet to cover another and enough brocade to cover a third. The cost was £44.15.10*d* (£44.79) equivalent today to around £3,800. Such a sum was greater than the average annual earnings at the time. The author was amused to see that a Miss Armstrong was also a customer. Her purchases however were rather more modest – a mohair dress costing £2.2.0*d* (£2.10) and a dozen cambric handkerchiefs at 1/9*d* (9p) each. Prices in those pre-decimal days tended for small items to be in farthings. Many readers will recall from holidays in Italy in the pre-Euro days with the smallest item costing thousands of lira that small change was often in the form of caramellos. W. J. Aldiss was ahead of that game, giving safety pins for change in lieu of coppers!

Mr Val had two sons. The elder, William James (Bill), joined Palmer's in Great Yarmouth to learn the business and later, at Bettys of Holt, had great success building the outdoor and sporting clothing side of the business, but died at an early age, leaving his younger sibling, Tim, to take up the reins. After a spell working on a farm 'Mr Tim' joined the business, but it wasn't until 1966 that he became a director. He recalls that he had his mother to thank for this appointment – apparently she kept telling Mr Val that it was high

Pins used as small change.

Queuing outside the Aldiss store, 1940s.

time Tim was appointed to the board. 'Mr Tim' became managing director in 1988, and soon the main Aldiss store moved into its new superstore, in a former printing works – quite a story in its own right and explained later.

In the 1940s the times had been difficult enough, and queuing was accepted by a generation to whom it had become the norm. Through the generations the Aldisses have proved themselves adept at responding quickly to market opportunities; being simply 'Drapers and Milliners' was not enough. Mr Val had the courage to seek to expand even in such austere times, and purchased the long-established store, Betty's of Holt, in 1947, which sold fashion. He then added H. B. Moulton, a traditional 'Gentlemen's Outfitter & Hatter' across the road, trading from Lion House. But the company also continued to grow organically, in particular by expanding its fashion department, a natural enough progression for a draper also selling millinery and haberdashery and with long experience in retailing dress materials. But the most important and permanent expansion was in the furnishing department. In the immediate post-war years stock was hard to come by and Mr Val responded by buying second-hand furniture at auctions which was then refurbished as necessary before being resold in the store. Tim Aldiss recalls that his father didn't just buy furniture at the sales, he bought widely, including the toys with which Tim and his brother grew up. At least he didn't repeat the buying practice of his father who, anticipating the First World War, stocked up to the hilt with items such as heavy black lisle stockings, only to be frustrated later by changing fashions! By the late 1930s a furnishing department was operating on the second floor of the Upper Market store. Retailing furniture has two characteristics which differentiate it from drapery. First, being able to display furniture to good effect requires a large floor area and, second, the staff ratio to turnover is much lower where the goods sold are items such as dining room suites rather than ribbons and hats. Both these differentiators have had significant impact on the development of the store. One lesson learned was that selling furniture from the second floor was not convenient, and soon warehouses had been acquired to facilitate the storage of large amounts of stock.

The need for space has resulted in a succession of moves of physical location, first to other family owned property on the Holt Road then to the disused Court House and later to premises made possible by the demolition of The Bell pub and some cottages. In 1969 part of this site was sold to the district council in anticipation of a road widening scheme. By 1989 the company had moved its furniture department into a former printing works, where the superstore is today. Fashion remained in the Upper Market and administration was carried out in a neighbouring building. At this time Tim Aldiss's father, 'Mr Val', was still alive and staff recall his visits to the store, accompanied by his nurse who pushed him in his wheelchair, like a real life Mr Grace.

Over the following years the property was extended and improved until today it houses all the Fakenham retail space, the administrative offices and a restaurant for the use of customers. The move to the present site was not entirely straightforward. The plan was first to develop the former Edmondson's garage site as a large new warehouse facility to free up more retail space, and this was carried through. But almost as soon as it had been, Tesco expressed an interest in buying the site for a new store. Always quick to react to fresh opportunities, Tim Aldiss purchased alternative accommodation for warehousing, and agreed to sell the former garage site. At this point Tesco had a change of heart and decided not to go ahead; Aldiss was left with two sites. For the moment the company stayed in the former garage site and held the other as an investment. They didn't have to wait long for it to pay off, and an agreement was reached for the garage site to be sold for housing development. Then things became complicated: Tesco had another change of heart and decided that they did want the site after all. A triangular game of commercial badminton ensued with the site passing between the players like a shuttlecock. The end result satisfied all three parties. For Aldiss, capital was released to facilitate new building and the end result was a superstore with excellent parking for customers. The former printing works was a property in which Tim Aldiss had expressed an interest before, but the agents seemed set on selling to the sitting tenants – a book company. He had had reason to be grateful to his mother for his directorship, now he had reason to be grateful to his wife, Penny. It was she who came up with the idea that he should negotiate with those sitting tenants to see if they would be interested in an early selling-on, at a profit. They were, and without the knowledge of the selling agents a further sale was agreed. Tim Aldiss recalls that the sale to the tenants was completed at 10.00 a.m. and at midday he completed the purchase from them. He rather enjoyed asking the agents for the keys to a property they had preferred to sell to someone else only that day. The purchase of this site was something of a risk – planning permission for the change of use might have been difficult but they discovered that the North Norfolk District Council were very positive; Fakenham, with the closing both of the print works and a number of other businesses was experiencing an increasing amount of unemployment and the prospect of new life and new jobs was, as Tim recalls, 'manna from heaven for the Council'.

The lower staff ratio necessary to sell furniture had also brought opportunities to experiment with new ideas. Tim Aldiss persuaded his father, who was initially doubtful about its wisdom, to adopt a different approach: the extensive use of discounting. The result totally vindicated Tim's approach. The rapid growth of turnover meant that even with a diminished margin the overall profitability was increased. Discounting became, and remains today, central to the Aldiss philosophy. If 'Pile it high and sell it cheap' was Jack Cohen's credo then 'Display it attractively and give value for money' more accurately reflects that of Aldiss. And discounting wasn't entirely new to the company. As early as 1912 W. J. Aldiss had been promoting his business by discounting, claiming that 'Tons of Ready-made Clothing, Boots and Shoes' were available for sale at 'Startling Low Prices'.

That expansion in fashion was a natural move. Although the company finally withdrew from this market in 2008, it was for many years a staple part of the business. During the 1960s Fashion parades were a regular feature at the store, and attracted many local housewives. But fashion is fickle, and forty years later it was clear to the management of the firm, by now strengthened by the recruitment of Paul Clifford as a non-family managing director, that times had changed. By 2008 the proportion of the company's turnover attributable to fashion was less than 5 per cent. It was time to reallocate resource to other product lines. By this time Tim Aldiss had moved over to take the chairmanship of the company, but he sought to reassure local residents that the family had no plans to sell its iconic premises. Indeed they were let to other retailers until the town was deprived of the splendid building by a disastrous fire some six years later.

Aldiss fashion parade, 1960s.

Aldiss fashion parade, 1960s.

By 2003 'Mr Tim' was looking to reduce his executive role a little and the store briefly became the responsibility of a management buyout team and a non-executive director. The loss of Tim's knowledge of retail meant that decision making was in less experienced hands. The team planned to leverage the goodwill it enjoyed in Norfolk by opening another store in Norwich in 2003, of a size comparable to its base in Fakenham. It was a capital intensive strategy and the belief that Aldiss enjoyed, in Norwich, the level of brand awareness it had in Fakenham proved a fallacy, despite regular advertising on local television and in the press. It was at that point that Jarrolds revived an old interest in purchasing the Aldiss assets. Their timing was good, and the approach was taken seriously. At first the discussions went well and, as it turned out, prematurely – the local press announced that it was 'a done deal' in June of that year. Little more than a month later it was clear that terms could not be agreed which would satisfy both parties, and the deal was off. These were not easy times for 'Mr Tim'. Still anxious to reduce his executive responsibilities he found himself with a new range of challenges to meet.

Tim Aldiss has two daughters who, together with his former wife, Penny, remain directors of the company today. One of his daughters, Arabella, is married to an investment banker, Eric Kump, also now a director. One of those with whom he had a connection was Rob Templeman, a highly respected figure in retail and, at the time, the chief executive of Debenhams. Briefed as to the challenges by Tim Aldiss, Eric Kump approached Rob Templeman, who arranged for a contact of his, Paul Clifford, to review the Aldiss business. Not a lot of grass grew under his feet; asked on Tuesday to do the review he gave his completed report to Templeman on Friday. It was shared with Tim Aldiss on Saturday and on Monday he was offered, and accepted, the challenge of becoming managing director of Aldiss, which he remains to this day.

During his time as managing director, Tim Aldiss had seen many changes, and initiated more. Expansion was significant – in the early years of the twenty-first century not only was the additional superstore opened in Norwich, but with an updated store in Fakenham, retail floor space approached 100,000 square feet. Much of the success can be attributed to the successful direct marketing campaigns instigated by the directors and their advertising agency. Recognising the changes in shopping habits, Aldiss's were quick to develop stores which were accessible to the motorist. Window shopping is not practical from behind the wheel of a car so the company took the stock to their potential customers in a very practical way with frequent mailings of well-illustrated catalogues and sale offers. Another change was that bad debt was dealt with more robustly. Tim Aldiss recalls pursuing one customer with a long-standing debt into the car park. Obviously the customer knew what was coming and was ready. Asked when he was going to pay up he reached into his pocket and pulled out a daisy chain of fivers which he had sellotaped to one another like a piece of bunting. For the rest, he offered Tim twelve whales' teeth (declined) or a supply of handkerchiefs, china and glassware. These were accepted and Tim claims this unusual means of settling a debt was what caused him to set up a department to sell them.

Paul Clifford has built significantly on Tim Aldiss's dependence on traditional non-internet based direct marketing. Despite a limited amount of television advertising targeting an audience with less general awareness of the Aldiss brand, associated by customers with value for money pricing and good service, most of the budget is split between product specific press advertising and a quarterly mailshot. The benefit of direct marketing is that, as is not the case with other forms of advertising, it is possible to measure accurately the returns. With a database of 80,000 warm existing customers responding positively to quarterly catalogues and discounts, a steady stream of repeat customers came through the doors. It is perhaps because of those brand values that the response rates to the regular mailings are so high.

Tim Aldiss always had an eye open for opportunities to promote both his business and the town that was its home, but he was astonished when, in 1986, one of his initiatives led to accusations that he was responsible for encouraging devil worship!

In 1982 he owned, in partnership with some friends, a store in Newmarket, and his partners there had employed the services of a clairvoyant to entertain their customers by giving Tarot readings in the shop, without charge. It had been a tremendous success at pulling in crowds and Aldiss felt that what worked on the flat in Newmarket would also work over the jumps at Fakenham, so he decided to replicate the event in his store. Naturally, to ensure the maximum coverage he made no secret of his plans, and there was plenty of advance publicity. But the response to this was mixed; he had been right – there was massive public interest. But there was an unexpected reaction from some members of the community. The local Baptist minister was horrified at the plan, and in somewhat immoderate language suggested in a letter to Aldiss that the event would be tantamount to encouraging 'devil-worship'. He went further, describing the Tarot cards as 'instruments of the devil'. His church treasurer joined the fray, telling the press that after thirty-three years as a customer of Aldiss she would hesitate to shop there again while money was spent on 'unhealthy pursuits'. By this time poor Tim Aldiss, who had been a sidesman at his local (Anglican) church, was feeling battered and not a little confused by all the fuss. He had meant to set up a harmless piece of fun for his customers, intended to encourage them into the store, entertain them while they were there and create wider interest in both the store and the town. He appeared instead to have started a holy war.

He certainly got more interest than he bargained for. The national press became involved and it was a gift for the pun-loving headline writers: 'Shoppers may be told what's in store' , 'Shoppers learn what fate has in store' and 'Better business on the Cards' were just three examples. The BBC picked up the story. Aldiss found himself being interviewed on Radio 4 and was quoted widely in the papers. *The Times* reported a proposed boycott of the store by the town's Baptists under the headline 'Baptists in 'evil' card warning'. The interest was even international; he was asked to comment on radio as far away as New Zealand. Perhaps the unkindest reporting was in *The Police Gazette* where the writer, having at some length explained the position under the requirements of the Vagrancy Act 1824, wrote that the Act was '(despite what is said in Butterworth's Police Law, page 376) not intended to allow any immunity to fortune tellers at fairgrounds and similar places'. He finished by expressing the hope that the clairvoyant would be both 'sent packing' and prosecuted. He was to be disappointed.

Tim Aldiss was in a predicament; loathe to lose the good will of those customers who were offended, he was equally anxious not to disappoint those who were looking forward to the event. His final decision was to go ahead with his plans. The event turned out to be a huge success with long queues waiting for their fortunes to be read. *The Times* reported that one customer had even travelled over 130 miles for his reading, and Aldiss, with great presence of mind, extended the event for a further day so that all those who wished for a reading could have one. Aldiss had been vindicated. As for the clairvoyant, Stephen Alexandre, he was able to book more sessions in the town the following week. Fakenham had been good for him, though perhaps Tim Aldiss wished that Alexandre's ability to foretell the future had stretched to warning him about the fuss that was to follow. Some storm, some teacup! It is something of an irony that, despite the success of the initiative, even thirty years later, and retired, Tim Aldiss still describes the incident as one he really regrets. 'I had no wish to offend anyone' he told me 'and I can still recall the sadness I felt when customers of thirty years standing, with whom I had always enjoyed a good relationship, wrote to say they would deal with the store no more'.

Like Palmer's (qv) Aldiss suffered an horrendous fire, but much later, in May 2014. As with Palmer's, the nature of the goods (including fabrics) on the premises accelerated the blaze. But, in contrast to the situation at Palmers more than 100 years earlier, the trading position of Aldiss was not affected as they were, by then, simply the landlords of what had once been their fashion store. It was in 2008 that the new professional management brought in by the Aldiss family concluded that, given the highly volatile nature of the fashion business and the intense competition, it no longer remained sense to compete as an independent in this market in a small Norfolk town. The freehold of the property belonged to another Aldiss company, A & B Management Services, who let the premises to another store. The fire was dramatic enough though. Tim Summers, the company secretary of both

Aldiss after the fire.

companies, recalls how he was called one Sunday morning while travelling and told the store was on fire. He hurried back to Fakenham, expecting to find a minor incident, only to discover, when miles away, that a huge pall of smoke was already visible over the town. Arriving at the site he was soon settled in the control unit established by the emergency services at a safe distance from the seat of the fire. Later he learned that the fire had been discovered about half an hour after the store opened. The store was quickly evacuated but one staff member, running one last check to make sure the first floor had been cleared, had to make her way out in choking smoke, and got clear of the building just minutes before the heat caused the windows to blow, sending shards of glass flying. The whole surrounding area was choked with smoke; a service in the parish church close to the scene had to be stopped as the church filled with smoke, and the congregation evacuated. Some of the neighbouring properties had residential accommodation in flats above the retail premises and two or three residents had to be rescued. It was little short of a miracle that no one was injured, but there were humorous moments: Tim Summers recalls that on his arrival at the control centre he found a case of small bottled water. As he said, it was quite a relief to discover that these were intended to slake the thirst of the firemen rather than being used to extinguish the fire! Neighbouring properties were affected too, but most were saved. Work on clearing the site continues and the plan is to rebuild as soon as practicable. The loss of such an attractive building leaves a large, if temporary, scar on the town.

Today Aldiss is a highly focused store, having rationalised its outlets to two superstores, in Fakenham and in Norwich, and specialising in the sale of furniture with other departments providing a wide range of homewares and gifts. Betty's of Holt no longer fitted the firm's strategy – it just wasn't large enough to stock the entire range of stock and was sold off to Bakers & Larners (qv). While internet shopping is available, furniture doesn't lend itself comfortably to this medium – returning a bed in a prepaid envelope is hardly practical if the buyer decides it isn't what he wanted; the policy remains to attract the customer to the store. The two superstores, both of them spacious and designed to show the suites and beds to their best advantage, have between them retail footage of around 90,000 square feet where the 179 employees generate a turnover of around £18 million a year. W. J. Aldiss may no longer promote itself as the 'People's Draper', but it has retained the knack of pleasing the people, with a combination of quality goods, competitive prices and excellent customer service.

Jarrold & Sons, Norwich

If you behave Rude and Affronting there is no hope of their Returning or their future Custom.

John Jarrold, 'His Book', on retaining customers

The assistant without a smile is incomplete

From Jarrold & Sons instructions to assistants, *c.* 1890

Partial Jarrold family tree showing the relationship of those mentioned in this chapter

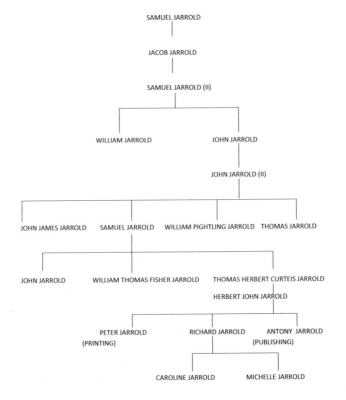

SAMUEL JARROLD

JACOB JARROLD

SAMUEL JARROLD (II)

WILLIAM JARROLD   JOHN JARROLD

JOHN JARROLD (II)

JOHN JAMES JARROLD   SAMUEL JARROLD   WILLIAM PIGHTLING JARROLD   THOMAS JARROLD

JOHN JARROLD   WILLIAM THOMAS FISHER JARROLD   THOMAS HERBERT CURTEIS JARROLD

HERBERT JOHN JARROLD

PETER JARROLD   RICHARD JARROLD   ANTONY JARROLD
(PRINTING)   (PUBLISHING)

CAROLINE JARROLD   MICHELLE JARROLD

Jarrolds store, *c.* 1909.

In the year 1823, Family Business being so depressed, I and my elder son came to Norwich and guided by our all wise benevolent providence, I with his personal assistance commenced a Bookselling, Printing and Binding business.

John Jarrold (II) in a letter to one of his younger sons, in 1845

Thus it wasn't until 1823 that Jarrolds became a Norfolk retailer, but its story goes back a lot further than that, to the mid-1700s, and those earlier days provide an important backdrop.

John Jarrold (II)'s grandfather, Samuel Jarrold (II), had run a grocery and drapers business in northern Essex and made a success of it. In the Jarrold family Christian names were often passed down from generation to generation, so it is sometimes necessary to distinguish between those of the same name by numbering them.

Samuel II had inherited property from his grandfather Samuel, his own father, Jacob, having died young; he made effective use of his inheritance, and when he died, in 1757, he was able to make good provision for his three sons. The main beneficiary was his eldest son William to whom he left the business, some property and £500 in cash. William swiftly augmented this by marrying an heiress, a Miss Bridgman, whose father was also in the retail business, in Woodbridge. His younger brothers had also benefited from their father's will, each inheriting £1,000.

William assumed responsibility for his brothers and arranged for one of them, John, to be apprenticed, aged thirteen, to William's father-in-law Thomas Bridgman as a grocer. John's character may well have been shaped under the influence of Bridgman, who took him firmly under his wing. John lived with Bridgman, who not only encouraged his involvement with the nonconformist chapel but helped him to develop in a commercial sense too.

John proved an apt and attentive pupil. He was a serious-minded young man and very attentive to his studies. He kept what he called his 'commonplace book', which he entitled 'John Jarrold, His Book'. He was clearly an observant boy and he set out in 'His Book' a set of rules for success in business. These were determined by what he described as the 'Rules of Decency', and included a commitment to be patient with difficult customers recording, 'if you behave Rude and Affronting there is no hope of their Returning or their future Custom'.

By the time he had reached the age of twenty-seven he had both the knowledge and the ambition to become a successful retailer. And at that age he acquired the means too, gaining access to the £1,000 his father had left him; he promptly invested this by buying a property in the Market Place at Woodbridge and setting up as grocer in his own right. What his old master, Bridgman, made of this new competition in the town is a matter of speculation.

Soon afterwards John married an Elizabeth Cranwell Coates who was from Lincolnshire but who had family in Norwich, and they set up home together in rooms above his new shop. They went on to have five children, four daughters and a son – John Jarrold II (JJ), who was later to open the shop in Norwich. But before that time there were many crises to overcome. John Jarrold senior died when he was only in his thirties and JJ was just two, and although the shop was then let there was no doubt that he would be expected to continue the family tradition of retailing.

His mother had a difficult relationship with her daughters. The exact nature of these is lost in the mists of time, but they were clearly significant as the daughters went to live with friends in Woodbridge. The blame seems to have been, at the time, placed on the mother, as she was excommunicated by her church on account of her behaviour to her daughters; she moved to Norwich, where by then her parents lived, taking her young son with her. JJ spent nearly ten years there, but then his mother also died and at twelve he went to live with his guardian John Bidwell, a draper in the city.

Bidwell was one of the two executors of Elizabeth's will, the other being an attorney called Charles Cooper, who was entrusted, unwisely as it transpired, with the family money. Cooper was an unreliable man who converted the money to his own use, buying himself an estate near Thorpe. It took JJ nearly thirty years to recover most of the money, and the story of this achievement could fill a chapter in its own right. Incidents such as the bailiff swooping late one foggy night on a coach in which the lawyer was leaving the city heavily muffled as a disguise, were followed by a series of extraordinary suggestions as to who might guarantee the lawyers payments when he agreed that he would settle up. These included a bankrupt, a man who was himself dependant on the lawyer and an 'unsafe man who kept women in the house'. At least he kept the matter out of Chancery or instead of just a chapter, the story might have become entangled enough to merit a book the length of *Bleak House*.

In the meantime JJ followed in his father's footsteps by becoming, at the age of fifteen, a grocer's apprentice. He was placed, in Stalham, with an Obadiah Silcock, who appears

John Jarrold (II).

either to have been a grocer or a wine merchant, perhaps a rather ironic choice since JJ later became an active temperance campaigner, though his maternal grandfather had also been a wine merchant. Like his father, JJ proved a quick and able pupil. He showed particular promise with figures, one example being his very precise calculation of the debt of the lawyer Cooper to the exact penny.

His apprenticeship over, JJ remained working in Stalham with Obadiah Silcock, who had been very impressed with him. In fact Silcock later gave him a reference, describing him as 'sober, honest and industrious' and as 'a responsible person in whom confidence could be placed'. But JJ was nothing if not ambitious and he entered, at the age of twenty-two, into a partnership with Richard Bidwell, the son of his guardian, in a traditional Norwich business – the manufacture of shawls and scarves.

The partnership only lasted three years and its dissolution provided him with some capital which, together with the first repayments from Cooper, gave the freedom to invest in his father's Woodbridge business to which he had returned a year earlier in 1797, marrying Hannah Hill, a childhood friend, the same year. They were to have four sons and one daughter; while the daughter sadly died in infancy, all four sons survived and each was to become a major player in the family business.

The eldest son, John James, was born in 1803 and in the meantime the business in Woodbridge progressed with JJ adopting many of the practices of his father, as set out in that commonplace book – 'prompt payment of debt, proper accounts, fair dealing and never either to borrow or lend'. These practices stood him in good stead with his suppliers who, confident that he would pay promptly, gave him keen prices enabling him to be competitive. From the outset he had shown his mettle. In 1797 he announced his arrival by printing a handbill which announced the sale of old stock at 'prime cost and under' and promised a restocked shop in every department and his 'determination to sell every article on the lowest terms'. And it wasn't just retailing that demanded his attention. He was a true entrepreneur and, seeing that the Napoleonic Wars had sent food prices soaring, he bought a farm near Woodbridge to take advantage of the opportunity for profit. When the war ended, the situation changed: prices fell and the farm became less profitable.

Change was needed and JJ had the wit to see it. A major, if slightly fortuitous, move into printing and publishing in which he already had an interest was facilitated by the decision of his brother-in-law, with whom he had been in partnership, to move out of printing and into the production of printer's ink. Luckily the outbuildings at the farm provided accommodation for the presses. The early titles, listed in a catalogue of 1818, were predominantly of a religious or 'improving' nature; hymns and psalms jostled with collected sermons and 'Entwistle's Essay on Secret Prayer'. 'Two Conversations between a Father and Daughter on Christian Baptism' was listed with educational material such as 'Captain Cook's Voyages Round the World' and a series of tracts to inform and 'improve' the newly literate working class. Thus began the remarkable success story of Jarrolds as printer and publisher. Remarkable as that story is in its own right it has no place in this chapter about the retailing interests, and these were not of a scale to satisfy JJ, who began to look for a larger market in which to practice the skills he had honed in Woodbridge.

Norwich must have seemed an obvious answer to him – a city he knew well from his childhood, and which, though declining as its traditional weaving and textile businesses contracted, still offered a much greater opportunity than was available in Woodbridge. So it was that JJ set out with his eldest son in 1823 determined to make a splash. With him he took, so family tradition has it, not just his son but £7,000 in cash. One feels the decision to take cash, equivalent today in inflation terms to well over £500,000 must have been an example of 'dressing to impress'. It was certainly not the safest thing to do. Gurney's Bank, where he opened an account on his arrival, had discovered the dangers themselves when their employee, Mr Mottram, travelling to London with a cargo of specie, had met with a highwayman who made three attempts to stop the coach. On the third pass another passenger spotted a metallic object in the highwayman's hand which he took to be a pistol, and shot the man dead. The metal object turned out to be a candlestick.

If carrying so much cash was a ploy, it was a successful one. The Jarrolds rapidly acquired premises on Cockey Lane (now London Street) very close to where the store is today, and opened, initially, as booksellers and stationers. JJ had heard of the premises through the good offices of Obadiah Silcock, and he took a lease at a rent of £120 per annum. From the start the new business prospered; its location, just by the junction with the marketplace, already lit by gas, could not have been bettered and JJ found his policies of prompt payment and keen prices worked just as well on the larger stage that Norwich provided. On this larger stage he was able to target particular segments, and identified schools as key customers, a policy which was to be of benefit to the company for many years.

By 1825 he had already extended his stock in trade to include 'Magazines, Reviews and all other periodical publications, Account Books made to order, genuine patent medicines, music and musical instruments' a fairly eclectic mix to meet the needs of Norwich's growing population of around 40,000. Success was immediate. In 1828 the lease was renewed and by 1837 Jarrold's had acquired the freeholds of premises in Exchange Street, London Street and Cockey Lane at a total cost of around £8,700. By 1830 Jarrold's were advertising a vast range of products, from 'Asses' Skin Memorandum Books' to 'Violin Strings; English and Roman', and from 'Eton Latin Grammars' to 'Mathematical Instruments'.

Education remained a key market with a vast range of dictionaries, grammars, primers, and spelling books. Slates were in stock, as were slate pencils, pens, nibs, and penknives. Relaxation was catered for by the availability of battledores (racquets used in an elementary version of badminton) and playing cards. The last sits strangely with Jarrold's expectations of those moving on from school in to apprenticeships – as late as 1868 their apprenticeship contract still demanded of the apprentice that 'Fornication he shall not commit, nor matrimony contract, taverns and inns he shall not haunt. At cards, dice, or other unlawful games he shall not play'.

During this period his eldest son, John James Jarrold, worked closely with his father, and, in keeping with a family tradition of total abstinence, was one of the first in Norwich to sign the pledge despite the fact that some of his father's money was from the estate of JJ's maternal wine merchant grandfather.

Norwich Marketplace, *c.* 1850.

JJ's relationship with John James was excellent, but other family relationships became strained when his younger sons followed him to Norwich. He did not have the same faith in them as he had in John James. In particular he clashed with Samuel, perhaps the one with whom he had most in common, especially in their strong commitment to the temperance movement. In fact he wrote later of Samuel that 'it would have been far better had he gone from home as an apprentice journeyman under an intelligent Master for improvement and to be accustomed to a proper degree of subordination. Learning not to lord it over others, or think more highly of himself than he ought to think'. The other sons, William Pightling and Thomas, were little more in favour and it was only the soothing influence of John James that kept JJ matters relatively civil; even then communication was generally via John James.

John James was a strong advocate for his brothers. It was he who persuaded JJ to change the name of the business from 'Jarrold & Son' to 'Jarrold and Sons', but the extra 's' meant little to JJ. He seemed to regard it just as a piece of window dressing to keep the boys quiet. As far as he was concerned the business was his, though he acknowledged the help of John James. The business continued to perform strongly despite the fractious relationship between father and sons. Additional premises were acquired and the business expanded rapidly, largely on JJ's initiative, but his wife's death in 1840 was followed just three years later by that of John James. The latter's death meant the end of the buffer between father and younger sons and the deteriorating relationship must have been clear to staff – the two generations now communicated only in writing and, on at least one occasion, orders issued by one generation were countermanded by the other. Thomas Jarrold later referred to one such incident, describing how his father had wanted some alterations made and had employed a carpenter by the name of Brooks to carry them out. As Brooks was about to begin work he was challenged by Samuel who said that as Brooks had only been instructed by one partner and not by the other three, the work was not to go ahead, and Brooks was 'immediately sent home'.

The younger generation were full of ideas for development; JJ regarded them as dangerous, inclined to overstock and as he pithily put it, 'useless'. For the boys part they saw their father simply doing as he wished, with no consultation. Worse, he was taking money out of the business for personal investment and cutting back the time he committed to the running of the business. Also, he seemed mean – the combined pay of his sons was, on his own admission, less than he donated annually to charity. The problem can be quite simply stated: they believed they were partners in the business, he did not.

Although the business was still prospering there were several reasons why the situation could not be allowed to continue. First, the money being removed by JJ to fund personal investment reduced the amount available to invest in the business. Second, the clear disparity of view and lack of communication between the generations not only meant that it was impossible to develop an agreed strategy, but also that even at a tactical level there was no agreement. Finally, the lack of rapport was inevitably, if sustained for long, going to impact on the morale of staff, confused as they must have become by contradictory instructions.

Strangely, as long ago as 1830 JJ had advised his eldest son that as 'I find my own health within the last year considerably diminished ... I am desirous gradually to withdraw from the responsibility and fatigue of business'. Clearly he felt invigorated (or contrary) enough to continue, although in December 1844 a document was prepared by William Pightling Jarrold for his father's signature. This read, 'I have this night given and do hereby give up to my three sons all right and interest I might have claimed in the business carried out by us as booksellers etc. in London Street, Norwich. And I do hereby give up to them, my three sons, all my right and interest in the stock, Book debts etc.' JJ did not sign. His expressed willingness back in 1830 to cede the business to all his sons (but primarily to John James) had been dependent on a proper stocktaking being completed. It wasn't, and it seems possible that this failure may have been the cause of his belief that his younger sons had a tendency to overstock.

Something had to give, and it was the young Turks who set change in motion. Taking advantage of one of their father's increasingly frequent absences at his farm near Woodbridge, they got hold of the books, to which they were normally denied access, and took them, in 1846, with an explanation of their position and concerns, to an independent reviewer.

They made a good choice – a lawyer called Jacob Tillett. Tillett was a man of the highest standing, a prominent Liberal who was well known to Thomas Jarrold, who, together with him and others, including Jeremiah Colman, had the previous year established a newspaper called the *Norfolk News*, which in time became the *Eastern Daily Press*. Although Tillett was of a different generation than JJ, he was only twenty-eight when asked to investigate the Jarrold's situation; he was acknowledged by JJ to be a person in whose 'discriminating ability to understand the business, and his wish to decide impartially' he could place 'full reliance'. This was just as well because when Tillett expressed the view that the sons had in fact been entitled to be treated as full partners since 1830, when the name had been changed to include them he admitted that he had arrived at the decision more as a matter of equity than by strict interpretation of the law. Perhaps surprisingly JJ, though he refused to acknowledge Tillett's conclusions as anything more than 'an opinion', accepted the inevitable and wrote 'the business I yield to my sons, therefore entirely given by me to them with the hope I shall to the end of my life secure their affection and goodwill'. Shortly afterwards he sold his livestock and let his Woodbridge farm to provide himself with an income in retirement. Many years later, in 1924, Jarrold's published a rather sanitised history of the business entitled 'The House of Jarrolds', which summarised the story in a single, understated sentence: 'Mr Jarrold retired from the partnership, leaving the business to his three surviving sons.'

Released from the constraints they had been experiencing, the three brothers concentrated on growing the business. One of their first acts was to agree to draw only a modest salary; in fact none of them drew more than £170 per annum in the first thirteen years of their management. They were to prove that the 'useless' tag with which their father had anointed them was far from the truth.

The business, of course, was far more than just the store and although this chapter is about the retail arm of the business, it's worth noting that the brothers invested significantly in new printing plant and in a new office in London to take advantage of the opportunities offered by improving standards of literacy among the general population. Publishing was a major element of their success. Of the three brothers it was Thomas who had particular success in this field. It was he who decided to publish the children's book *Black Beauty*, written by Anna Sewell, the daughter of Mary Sewell, one of the more prolific writers of those 'improving' tracts which Jarrolds published to encourage the newly literate working class. *Black Beauty* was not particularly well received by other booksellers – the number taken by London booksellers originally was only around 100 between them. But Jarrolds, who had developed a strong relationship with schools made hay and Thomas's faith in the quality of the book paid dividends.

The three brothers continued to work together until 1874 when Samuel, the brother perhaps closest in temperament, if most distant in terms of relationship to his father, died unexpectedly. JJ, who had died in 1852, just six years after retirement, would, despite his general poor opinion of Samuel, have appreciated Samuel's devotion to the cause of temperance. Samuel habitually set out early in the morning with a set of tracts hidden in his tall hat, which he distributed to working men he encountered. It was in doing work of this nature for the advancement of temperance that he caught the chill which led to his death. And now there were two, but not for long – it was just two years later that his brother William Pightling died, childless. And then there was one, but for an even briefer period – Thomas died just a year later.

After the deaths of Samuel and William, Thomas had run the business with his nephew Samuel John James, generally known as John, the eldest son of the late Samuel. John was in an invidious position. With the death of his uncle Thomas he was running the business alone, but he did not have any share of the ownership – he was simply a salaried manager. This position arose because his father had left his estate to be shared between his widow, who was John's stepmother, and his sister in law, the wife of Thomas. His stepmother, who had met Samuel at a temperance meeting, was ambitious for the two sons born to her and Samuel, John's half-brothers, and was hostile towards John. A state of cold war prevailed for more than ten years, at which time his aunt, the widow of Thomas, offered John her share of the business, which he bought with the help of a mortgage of £5,000 (around £500,000 in today's values).

But the long struggle with his stepmother had impacted on John's health and he died just two years later at the age of forty-two. His stewardship of the company had been excellent. The extent of the development of the store under his management was clear from a publication in 1891, just a year after his death, which was fulsome in its praise for the shop, which had been transformed into a model department store:

In London Street there are 2 splendid shops, one devoted to books and stationery and the other to travellers' requisites, trunks, portmanteaux, Gladstone bags, toilet cases, ladies' dress baskets etc. all of the newest type and best manufacture........beneath the stationery shop is a commodious store for paper and ink; while from the trunk shop, by a handsome staircase we descend to a spacious bazaar for the sale of art, pottery and glass of every description.......at the rear of the bookshop are several departments, each having its own particular showroom, well lighted and furnished with handsome showcases. These departments comprise cricket, lawn tennis, golf and similar goods .... fancy leather goods, such as purses, writing cases, dressing cases etc. and a third for mounted and un-mounted photographs, albums, fancy articles of all kinds, brass ornaments.....Adjoining is a library, well stocked with works

Jarrolds shop front and reading room, *c.* 1900.

of all descriptions. In the Exchange Street premises there are also two shops - the magazine and stationery department and the second hand bookstall. For the convenience of customers there is, on the first floor of the London Street premises a reading room, well-furnished and supplied with papers and periodicals.

On the second floor was a circulating library, with an annual subscription of 14/6d. Later a newsroom was added where citizens could catch up on what was happening – there was 'a constant stream of telegrams from all parts of the world'. Day tickets were available to non-subscribers. In keeping with the strong nonconformist Jarrold tradition, there was also a 'Bible Room', and, more intriguingly, an 'Assistants Unrobing Room'!

The premises were physically integrated, but this arrangement was not without its problems. In 1902 the Diocesan Surveyor was employed to value the properties, concluding his valuation with a dire warning: 'I feel it my duty to call your attention to the terrible havoc that would take place should a fire occur, and the little chance of confining it to the neighbourhood of the outbreak ...' Clearly the time was approaching when major changes to the physical nature of the store would be needed.

It was in this period that the Jarrolds started to expand their retail interests by opening branches: Cromer, opened in 1881 and still going strong today, was quickly followed by Sheringham, Yarmouth and Lowestoft, though these latter branches were closed, mostly in the 1960s and 1970s as the competitive environment became increasingly tough.

But other things were changing too, especially the approach to staff. In 1875 one young man named Hazell had been bound apprentice to Jarrold and Sons to learn the art of bookselling. For the privilege his father had paid Jarrolds a premium of £40 and promised to provide his son with 'sufficient good clothing, lodging, washing and other necessaries'. Hazell was to be paid 2 shillings a week for the first year of his apprenticeship, 3 shillings for the second, 4 shillings for the third, and 5 shillings for the fourth and final year, such pay to be suspended during any absence, for sickness or any other reason. The young man had himself to give certain undertakings. The moral constraints referred to earlier were supplemented with a requirement to 'do no damage to his Masters' and 'keep their lawful commands'.

By 1891 attitudes had softened somewhat. It was in that year that Jarrolds agreed to an experiment – half-day closing. For a trial period of one year it was agreed that the store would close at 2.00 p.m. on Thursdays in the summer months. Fifty-four employees signed a declaration that read, 'We, the undersigned, hereby promise that in the event of Jarrold and Sons deciding to close their establishment at London and Exchange Streets, Norwich, on Thursday afternoons at two o'clock during the months of May, June, July and August we will, on our part, do our utmost to cooperate with them in preventing the business of the firm suffering in any way as a consequence of this concession'. They also agreed that the experiment was for one year only and that on Thursdays there would be no lunch break. In this context the word 'lunch' really meant a mid-morning break.

On joining, an assistant was required to sign an agreement that he or she would clock in, leave their outer garments in the cloakroom, be at their counter before opening time and clock out at the end of the day. They were to be entitled to a break of forty-five minutes for 'dinner' (lunch) and twenty-five minutes for tea. They could also take a twenty-five-minute break for 'lunch' (elevenses), but if a customer wished to see them they must be summoned back 'at once' and 'under no circumstances' was the customer to be told that they were 'at lunch'. Any discrepancy in the cash balance of the till was to be made good at the joint expense of the assistant and the person responsible for checking individual payments. Staff were entitled to a 10 per cent discount on goods purchased, and if they paid all their bills for such purchases then an additional 5 per cent would be allowed at the year end. Two weeks holiday were allowed a year, and as that approached it must have been easier for staff to heed the exhortation in their instructions 'The assistant without a smile is incomplete'.

At the time, Jarrold's, in common with most other large stores, provided accommodation for some of their counter staff, but unlike some others this was not on the shop premises but in two other properties, The Lodge and the Chantry. The doors were locked at 10.30 p.m. in winter and thirty minutes later in summer. Apprentices were required to be in by 9.30 p.m. all year, perhaps to reduce their opportunities to breach the behavioural terms of their contracts! Late passes had to be approved by a director and the housekeeper, and 'sleeping out' was not allowed except with the special approval of the directors and a pass obtained from the secretary.

Jarrolds had long offered staff some form of annual entertainment; in 1900 this comprised a trip by rail to St Olave's, though the faces in the formal group photograph are sombre enough to suggest a funeral rather than a celebration. Family occasions were marked with staff events as well; Mrs Samuel hosted an event at the Agricultural Hall to celebrate William's wedding, to which she invited 260 staff.

The beneficiaries of all John's efforts had been his half-brothers, William Thomas Fisher Jarrold (William) and Thomas Herbert Curteis Jarrold (Herbert). To them fell the responsibility for acting on the warning given by the Diocesan Surveyor about the dangers of the building. To undertake the redevelopment of the store they employed George Skipper, a much respected Norwich architect, but first, in 1902, they changed the basis of the business from a partnership to a limited liability company. The sale of shares in the company helped to fund the cost of the improvements. William and Herbert took up all the Ordinary Shares, but £60,000 of debentures and £35,000 of Preference Shares were offered through Barclay's and fully taken up within ten days. The Prospectus gives an accurate picture of the staffing levels at this time: 370 in Norwich, divided almost equally between the store and the printing business, and a further sixty-five at Great Yarmouth, and, in the branches at Cromer and Sheringham respectively, nine and six.

George Skipper was an architect renowned for his flair, if not for his punctuality. On a number of occasions he had to be jockeyed along by WTFJ when he appeared to be falling behind the agreed dates and, on one occasion, must have caused considerable offence because Jarrold wrote to Skipper's brother, threatening to bar him from the premises : 'We must take the most serious objection at expressions and actions of your brother.....we hope he will have the good sense not to repeat his conduct for if he does we shall be most reluctantly obliged to ask you that he does not come on our premises.' Disappointingly there seems now to be no information available as to the cause of this disagreement. The delays and irritations were worth it. Skipper's work on Jarrolds was described by Pevsner as 'baroque'. Skipper's own office adjoined the Jarrolds' premises and later became a part of the store so that its terracotta panels, including likenesses of his own family, now form part of Jarrolds' façade. The overall effect of Skipper's work was to give an air of confidence in a prosperous future – and so it transpired. The work in Norwich was carried out by a builder called Thomas Gill, who won the contract by competitive tender, his quotation being £7,174 (around £750,000 in 2014 values).Under the joint management of William and Herbert the business, in all its manifestations, continued to prosper and the brothers were able to extend the property holdings of the company both in Norwich, and in Lowestoft.

During this period the retail business grew steadily, but the First World War brought difficulties. Quite apart from the impact of shortages on the printing side, the store was affected too. Book sales dropped dramatically, to such an extent that in 1915 Herbert Jarrold wrote to a previously successful author to tell him that only one copy of his book had been sold in the previous six months. He went on: ' It is difficult to realise how disastrous the War has been on the sale of books except those connected with the War itself......There is not a single book we have prepared for last Autumn's sale which has justified itself'. It wasn't just to the level of sales that the war brought change. As conscription took hold the company had to look to recruit more young women, and letters were sent to pupils as potential recruits. Schoolchildren were still catered for in the early days of the war, Santa Claus making a visit to the store at Christmas 1914, arriving in a horse-drawn coach rather than a reindeer-propelled sleigh. It was during the war that

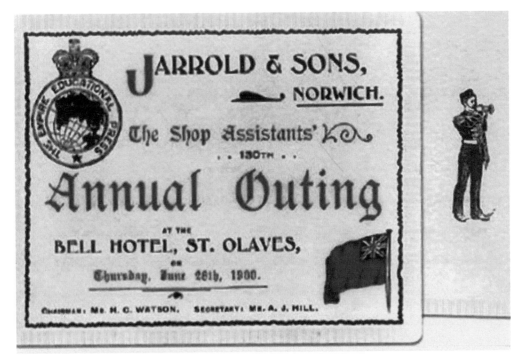

Staff outing invitation, 1900.

The staff pictured on their outing.

George Skipper's design for Jarrolds.

Jarrold's first provided motorised transport for its representatives, at this stage on two wheels.

As the war ended and the remaining men returned, Jarrold's began to expand again with an additional branch at Cambridge and further extension to the flagship store. The centenary of its establishment in Norwich was celebrated by the production of a short and rather sanitised book on its own history. The celebrations involved staff, who received an invitation:

> The Chairman and Directors
> Request the pleasure of the company of employees
> For Dancing, Music and Whist at St. Andrew's Hall

The event was held on the 11 January 1924 and planned to the last detail, even the dancing was predetermined. There were only to be three waltzes, and three 'one-steps', but six foxtrots. The dancing was to be supplemented with a performance by a concert party, a fancy-dress parade and the inevitable speeches. In that year the profit reached £8,000. The shop salaries totalled £18,300 – roughly three times what they had been in the late Victorian days.

At around the same time a restaurant was opened in the flagship store. The store itself was largely rebuilt, one feature being a splendid new 'arcade' entrance, which featured in a

Santa arrives at Jarrolds, 1914.

contemporary press advertisement. By this time the transport provided for representatives had moved to four wheels.

The store premises were kept under the watchful eye of Arthur (Joe) Dunham, the caretaker who, with his wife and daughters, lived in accommodation on the roof of the London Street store, where he created a magnificent garden, incorporating both a formal rose garden and a pond.

It was in 1927 that Herbert John Jarrold, 'Mr John', joined the business, first to work in it and then to manage it through some astonishing times. Although his main emphasis was on printing, retail was in his bloodstream, on both sides: his mother Mabel was a member of the Curl family whose store in central Norwich, destroyed by enemy action in 1942 and not rebuilt until fourteen years later, was eventually taken over and became part of Debenhams. Before that, Jarrold's, well managed and well diversified, coped better than most with what Auden called the 'low, dishonest decade' of the 1930s with the depression and then the spectre of war. During this period staff continued to enjoy regular outings – in 1934 Jarrold's kept up spirits at Christmas with a splendid Toy Fair. Many readers may, as I do, have memories later, in the 1950s, of happy post-Christmas hours spent in the toy department at London Street making the critical decision on how best to spend the Christmas Postal Order from a favourite uncle.

When war came it soon meant a severely reduced range of product offerings, and when Curl's was bombed out, Jarrold's were quick to make a floor available to their competitor. This early (and non-strategic) example of 'a shop within a shop' is ascribed by Mr John's son Mr Richard to a then prevailing attitude of cooperative rivalry. Jarrolds store in Yarmouth (left) also suffered bomb damage but could be repaired. In Norwich firewatchers were on duty in the store – one employee's entry in the fire-watch book complains that the chimney smoked 'like a curry house'.

When wartime shortages eventually began to recede the whole nature of retailing started to change, and has barely stopped changing since. Competition became increasingly fierce as the larger national companies moved into Norwich, opening new stores or acquiring existing local businesses, but Jarrold's continued independently.

Through the 1950s Jarrolds store had continued to flourish largely by sticking to its traditional methods, and the Coronation of Queen Elizabeth II was marked in style. Later Herbert's three sons, Peter, Richard and Antony, all joined the business. Peter's prime responsibility was for printing, Antony's for publishing, and it was the middle son Richard (RJ) who in time became responsible for the store. RJ joined the company in 1958, having spent some time training with Beales of Bournemouth, another old established independent store, one of whose claims to fame is to have been the first store to employ a 'real life' Father Christmas. The appearance of the Jarrolds store RJ joined had changed little since the war. He recalls that the wooden floors still had to be oiled regularly and that a pneumatic tube system was still in place for the handling of cash and change. Management information was thin on the ground – he recounts how sometimes it was only when an author pointed out to staff that no copies of their books were on the shelf that the work was reordered. Jarrolds was a fine traditional store offering a very personal service, but not perhaps fully prepared for the battle developing in the high street as the multiples stepped up their ambitions in the provincial cities.

Above left: Advertisement for Jarrolds Restaurant, *c.* 1924.

Above right: Artist's impression of Jarrolds Arcade, *c.* 1925.

Poster for Jarrolds Toy Fair, 1934.

That lack of accurate and timely management information in the 1950s and 1960s to which RJ alluded was addressed by the purchase of the firm's first computer, in 1969. Rather endearingly the *Jarrold Magazine* for January that year recorded that 'computers are so new that most firms are, like us, still learning to use them'. Initially payroll data was to be transferred onto the new system but it was 'a possibility' that better stock information could be produced as well. The description of the process for handling sales described in the Christmas 1968 edition of the *Jarrold Magazine* showed that some of the processes RJ had witnessed on his arrival were as yet unchanged, especially in the handling of sales:

All the tubes from the store come to the cash desk. This is a glass partitioned part of the cash office. Two or three girls may be working in front of open tills, receiving the cups from the tubes, checking in cash and giving change. Finally the bills are rubber stamped by the assistant showing their particular number.......the cups rattle up faster than can be dealt with. An urgent call for help is made to the outer office.....this goes on endlessly. At about 4 o'clock the tills are over-flowing and handfuls of money have to be taken out for counting ready for checking and cashing-up.

The arrival of computerisation must have been very welcome.

But the installation of the computer was not the only significant change in the 1960s. Over the years Jarrolds had gradually expanded, acquiring additional space as the opportunities arose. One significant site was the Norwich Corn Hall. Dating from the 1820s this had served not only as venue for the sale and purchase of corn but also as a place of entertainment.

Jarrolds, decorated for the Coronation, 1953.

Installing the first computer.

Both Liszt and Paganini had performed there, the latter causing some controversy. His performances in the corn hall were on the 28 and 29 July 1831 prior to a further engagement at the Theatre Royal. He did not please everyone and it seems likely that the charges he made were responsible for the *Norfolk Chronicle* describing him as a 'fascinating but by no means fair minded foreigner'. For the more low brow there was entertainment too. In the 1940s and '50s the hall had been the site for boxing matches. In September 1946 Charlie White, a Norwich featherweight, had beaten an Irishman … on points. That was unusual for White, whose bouts habitually ended in knockouts; more than two thirds of both his wins and his defeats ended that way. Later the hall became the venue for wrestling matches. In 1963 the market moved out of the city and Jarrolds were quick to snap up the premises.

It was a time when there was much emphasis on out of town shopping developments, so this expansion was somewhat against the trend. Coincidentally, as the negotiations continued RJ was in New York, where Macy's executives told him that they believed the future of retailing lay in out of city centres. He kept his own counsel and may have been tempted to give an enigmatic smile. If so would it surely have broadened into a wide grin as, in remarkably short order, Jarrolds opened in its extended premises with a brand-new fashion department. Macy's, of course, had only been around since 1858 so Jarrold's had the benefit of nearly an extra century of experience!

Fashion proved a huge success for the company. In a typical example of the way in which the Jarrolds sought to involve their staff as part of an extended 'family group', the new department was reviewed by two staff members. They reported enthusiastically in the *Jarrold Magazine* on the Mary Quant designs, the mink coats, the pearl-studded evening gowns and, rather more down to earth, they referred to the crimplene separates and the 'chunky bedsocks'.

Reading issues of the *Jarrold Magazine* of this era shows that the company exemplified that benevolent paternalism which still characterised the better employers at the time, but which is not generally so evident today. Jarrold's looked after its staff: from children's parties, through family sports days, staff dances and dinners and pensioner's outings, Jarrolds proved themselves caring employers on a near 'cradle to grave' basis. That kind of paternalism, so rare – and sometimes mocked today – was really an example of decent employers treating decent employees with respect and by doing so earning their affection and loyalty. In true traditional style Jarrolds presented gold watches to staff members achieving forty (later twenty-five) years service.

Not everything they did would today be seen as 'politically correct'. One of the features of the Children's Sports Day was the selection of the 'Jarrold Queen' who would, in her year of office, represent the company at various functions. To encourage participation the company offered a guinea to each contestant for a 'hair-do', but insisted that the contestants did not wear 'bathing costumes' when paraded before the judges! A prize (by 1968 it was £20) was offered for the winner, with smaller prizes for the runners-up. It may not have been politically correct in today's terms but it probably added to the fun of an essentially family day with a Punch and Judy show, tennis, football, races, Bingo and ice cream on sale 'all afternoon'.

Meanwhile the store, by now under RJ's direction, continued to prosper. Special events were a feature, with Douglas Bader one of those who did a signing session in the books

Fashion parade at Jarrolds.

department. But the greatest range of special events was reserved for 1970, when the whole company celebrated its bicentenary in style.

The celebrations opened on 01 May at Wymondham, where Antony Jarrold and his guests boarded a stagecoach for the journey to Norwich, having first lunched on Boars Head, Pumpkin Pie and 'Frefh Fruit'. All were dressed in period dress. Driving to Norwich they were accosted by a highwayman who relieved them of a (pre-prepared) haul then donated to a spastic charity. Two weeks later a specially chartered train brought a host of guests to Norwich for a guided tour, which was followed by a reception at the Castle Museum.

Of course this was a celebration for the whole company. The store celebrated with an eye-catching series of window displays and birthday cake served to customers taking tea in the restaurant. These were complemented with more than fifty special in-store promotions, special offers and competitions. It was a memorable year.

Twenty-five years later, as the store celebrated its 225th birthday, RJ reflected on the new challenges brought about by the increased competition as famous names moved into the new shopping malls. He was confident though of the future, expressing his determination that the store would retain its traditional family ethics and offering special value. And he was right, it has. Growth, both organic and by acquisition (for example of Pilch Sport in 2005), has helped. Twice it has been awarded the Drapers Magazine Independent Store of the Year Award.

In 2005 the company decided to focus its business on the retail store and the company's property portfolio, and sold the printing and publishing businesses. Retail, which is where

Jarrolds Queen finalists, 1968.

it all started back in 1770, has proved the most resilient of all the divisions. Despite the involvement now of some non-family members in the senior management of the company, one feels that John Jarrold would be delighted to know that two of his great-great-great-great granddaughers, RJ's daughters Caroline and Michelle Jarrold, are still part of that team too. It is Michelle who is involved with the retail side of the business, as its development director.

Bakers & Larners of Holt, Over Eight Generations

Let Aunts delight to bark and bite,
For God hath made them so;
Let all their nephews growl and fight,
For `tis their nature to
(With apologies to Isaac Watts, 1674–1748).

Partial family tree of the Baker family showing the relationship between those mentioned in the chapter

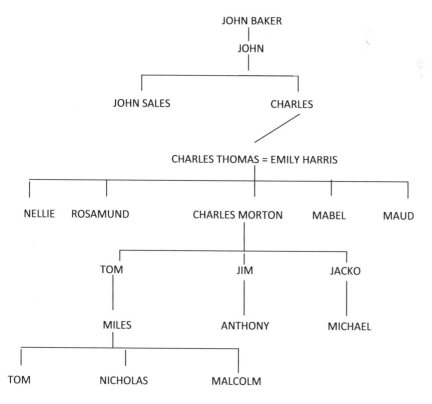

JOHN BAKER
|
JOHN
|
JOHN SALES — CHARLES

CHARLES THOMAS = EMILY HARRIS

NELLIE   ROSAMUND   CHARLES MORTON   MABEL   MAUD

TOM   JIM   JACKO

MILES   ANTHONY   MICHAEL

TOM   NICHOLAS   MALCOLM

*To promote a woman to bear rule, superiority, dominion or empire above any realm,
nation or city is repugnant to nature........it is the subversion of all order, of all equity and
justice ...*

When John Knox wrote those words in 1558 in his *First Blast of the Trumpet against the
Monstrous Regimen of Women* he might have added, in the case of C. T. Baker Ltd, the
word 'business' to 'realm, nation, or city'. At least that's how it must have felt to other
members of the family at the time when not one woman but four disharmoniously ruled
the roost at this long-established Holt business.

The firm traces its roots back to the early eighteenth century, though the evidence is
sparse. Adam Custance, a distant connection of the Custances of Weston Longville who
feature so frequently in Woodforde's diary, seems to have established himself in the town
as a joiner and ironmonger. Clearly he prospered, for his Will refers also to his being at
least the part owner of a ship. He died in 1782. Unusually for the time, he left a part of his
estate to his daughter, who was married to a John Baker. Baker took over the running of
the ironmonger's business, and the family connection can be traced with confidence back
to that date.

But antiquity alone was not enough to spare the business from the infighting of a
formidable quartet of ladies four generations later. These ladies were the great-great-
grand-daughters of John Baker. The period between Baker's death in 1804 and their
accession was one of growth in a succession of fits and starts.

Although John had eight children, only three outlived him – two sons and a daughter. Both boys attended Holt Grammar School (later Gresham's School) but clearly differed in their father's eyes. The elder, Adam Calthorpe, does not appear to have met with his father's approval. Having fathered an illegitimate child (John senior left provision in his Will for the child's maintenance) he was excluded from the role of executor, this task being left to his younger brother John, and his sister, Margaret.

The estate was not large; John (Senior's) effects were sworn not to exceed £600. A sum of £100 each was left to John and Margaret, the will making clear that Adam had enjoyed a similar benefit during the testator's lifetime. A further £100 was reserved to produce an income of 1/6d per week for the maintenance of 'the bastard child' of Adam, but the balance, including stock in trade, was to be left to the management of John (Junior) who was to ensure that his siblings each received a third of its value. He appears to have been ambitious. Until then the business had been carried on in rented premises, but he purchased freehold property with the help of a mortgage granted by his wife's uncle, Charles Sales, who owned a grocery and drapery business in Holt. Negative equity is not a new thing – Sales felt that the market value of the property might be less than the loan and, as a relatively wealthy man, he arranged to leave a sum to John to reduce the debt. Clearly even this was not enough as John later resorted to a technique characteristic of more recent times – a sale and leaseback. By selling the property to a Mr Muskett and renting at least a part of it back, he was able to continue trading from the same premises without the financial responsibilities of ownership. Although John lived to the age of ninety-two, he had retired some twenty-five years earlier in 1842, leaving the business to be run by his two elder sons who, at the date of his death, still owed him a little over £1,000, likely to have been the amount they were to pay for the business and its stock.

The two brothers, John Sales and Charles, were the third successive generation of Bakers to run the business, though Charles seems to have taken the most active part, and it was really under his management that the business began to grow and prosper. In the 1851 census he was described as an Ironmonger, employing four men, so the business was still relatively small. But it was also prosperous and Charles later lived in some style in Holt, employing both a governess for his children and two domestic servants.

As the business grew, Charles felt able to emulate his father and he started to buy the premises from which he traded, including a shop frontage of 22 feet. It seems possible that at this stage the business was expanding from simple ironmongery; as early as 1852 he bought additional space 'well adapted for a Grocer or general Shopkeeper', and though he later sold these premises to the Larner family, they were eventually to return to the Baker fold, as we shall see. In addition, Charles had interests in brewing and as a 'distributor of stamps', while his brother John, in his will, is described as a grocer and draper. The will was witnessed by Charles's son who was described as a draper. Perhaps the Baker family were already moving towards the much diversified trading model customers would recognise today.

Already the Bakers seem to have been seen as solid members of the community – three successive generations had served in the office of churchwarden and their dominance of trade within the town was becoming clear. All seemed set fair, and when Charles took his son Charles Thomas Baker into partnership in 1872, it was in anticipation of his own retirement five years later.

At this stage, inter-generational and familial relations seem to have worked well; there was none of the vituperation that was to follow when control fell into the hands of the deadlier of the species. In fact succession had been eased both in this instance and when Charles himself had inherited, by ensuring that the retiring parent enjoyed a 'pension' funded by the interest paid by the successor in respect of the amount owed to the retiree for the goodwill of the business passed over. In both cases this was not repaid until the death of the parent, easing the capital strain on the business while ensuring a steady income for the retiree.

Charles Thomas (CT) was a fortunate man. Not only did he inherit a thriving business, but he had married an Emily Harris, whose father was very comfortably off and willing to invest in his son-in-law's business expansion.

Thus provided for, CT began to acquire additional property in Holt, in Sheringham, and in Fakenham. In each town he developed his commercial activities. The scale of his achievement only becomes clear when one considers that it came at a time when the great agricultural depression was at its height. The development of railways and quicker sea passages meant a huge increase in competition for the provision of wheat and oats, bringing a sharp decline in the price. Wheat prices fell by more than 50 per cent in twenty years and agricultural workers left the land in droves, for the cities, for the colonies –

Charles Thomas Baker.

in fact for anywhere where there was the prospect of work and wages. Two thirds of Norfolk had been arable land as long ago as the start of the 1800s and the depression was particularly deep there.

While, by 1883, the role of Distributor of Stamps had moved to a Mr Preston, CT expanded into other fields. He was the agent for the Norwich Union, in which capacity he would have received 10 per cent of all premiums paid, and is listed in *Kelly's Directory* not just as an ironmonger and insurance agent, but also as a retailer of furnishings. White's Directory of the same year goes even further, identifying him as:

> Ironmonger, iron merchant, iron and template worker, brazier and bellhanger. Agricultural implement agent, oil and colour man, kitchen range, gas, hot water, pump worker & plumber, gunsmith, ammunition and fishing tackle dealer, and brick, tile, sanitary tube merchant; agent for the Norwich Union Fire and the Norwich Union Life Insurance Cos, the Norfolk Farmers' Cattle, the General Hailstorm, the Accident, the Norwich & London Accident and Casualty and Plate-Glass Insurance Cos.

Practically a one-man conglomerate!

His strategy seems to have been working: by then he was living in a spacious property, 'The Acacias' (now the Lawns Hotel). Meanwhile his uncle John Sales Baker was in business nearby as a grocer and draper, and his younger brother was listed as a brewer and wine and spirit merchant, in the High Street.

So great was the growth of the business that the workforce of four in his father's day had grown to thirty-seven by the time of CT's early death in 1900. His success came as a result of his personal qualities. Described by his cousin, a solicitor, as 'extremely able', he was known for an exceptionally hands-on approach to the whole range of business activity. He clearly didn't encourage initiative – nothing could be done except under his personal supervision.

While this high degree of focus paid dividends initially, it was to prove a disadvantage in the later years of his life when it would seem that deteriorating health may have affected his ability to control his growing empire. With initiative discouraged for many years there was no one qualified and willing to pick up the baton and the business did not enjoy its earlier success. Indeed by the time of his death the financial situation of the firm had become less robust – nearly half of the total assets were the subject of mortgages or debts, including nearly £3,500 owed to his widow.

CT had just one son, Charles Morton Baker (CM), who had become a solicitor, and five daughters. The eldest of these was Connie, whose poor health meant that she was never involved in the business, but her sisters later became embroiled in major disagreements about it. CM was behind the move to turn the business into a limited liability company, a course he had advised CT to adopt, but the latter's death occurred before the arrangements could be finalised. The company was incorporated three months later as C. T. Baker Ltd. The diversification away from simple ironmongery was explicitly acknowledged as the company was described as carrying on business as a 'Wholesale and Retail Ironmonger, Builder, Contractor and General Store'. CM had obviously worked quite hard on his father to secure his agreement to the change, but was frustrated by the delay caused by

Charles Morton Baker.

CT's failing health. His father's death left him effectively in operational charge of the business, a task for which he may not have been temperamentally suited. Ownership was a different matter. CT's widow whose family had, after all, been a source of capital to enable the company to expand, personally owned the freehold of the premises in Holt, Sheringham and Fakenham and held 5,000 shares in the company as well as a £5,000 4 per cent debenture, the latter two being effectively the price paid to her by the new company for the business.

She was also allotted one extra share and another share each was allotted to CM, his wife Mary and one of his sisters, Ros, and to three employees who became directors, John Richard Scoley as managing director, William Jabez Clarke, the manager of the works department, and Hiram Smith Watson, the manager of the Holt shop. Probably Ros was the only sister to benefit at that time, either because she was the only one to be actively involved at this stage in the business or because she was already showing that steely determination to have her own way which was to characterise her later management of the company.

CM's control of the business was not a great success. His mother's own solicitor later described him as 'quite inexperienced in commercial matters'. In fact he was by background a conveyancer and was town clerk of Sheringham; his contribution as company secretary, for which he was paid £75 per annum, was probably greater than that as its manager.

While he was running the business, returns fell and so did the dividends payable to the shareholders. There was some retrenchment and in 1903 the Fakenham business was closed. Within a couple of years CM had contracted pneumonia and died, leaving two infant sons, Tom and Jim. A further son, nicknamed 'Jacko', was born shortly after his death.

Initially control remained firmly with CM's mother Emily, who, as we have seen, was effectually the owner of the business. To the approbation of the staff members who had become directors on the establishment of the limited liability company, she made it clear, at the first board meeting following her son's death, that she intended the business to continue to be run in the same manner as before, but she brought in her own accountant and lawyer to advise her. The accountant, Mr Bishop, attended most of the board meetings that followed, and this may have been why, at the next general meeting (1905), action was proposed to address the continuing disappointing profit margin. Each of the director/employees was to submit monthly returns to Emily's solicitor, Mr Fisher. There was particular concern about the profitability of the works department and arrangements were made for separate accounts to be produced for that department so that its performance could be better assessed. Initially this seems to have coincided with an improvement in the performance of that department by 1908, possibly arising from building work for the expanding Gresham's School.

At the board meeting in January 1906, Emily had made a transfer of one share each to four of her daughters, thus opening the way for an era known to subsequent generations as 'the time of the Aunts'. Those familiar with the works of P G Wodehouse will know that, though they come in all shapes and sizes – lean and angular, short and stumpy, square-shaped or pear-shaped – the one thing that most aunts have in common is that they are very, very formidable. Bertie Wooster would have recognised at least one of the Baker aunts as belonging to that genre, at a hundred paces.

The Aunts

In the meantime though, things continued much as before, with profits affected by the corrosive effect of old and practically unsaleable stock, and the propensity of customers not to pay their bills promptly. As far as the stock was concerned, not only was control so poor that there were believed to be significant amounts not accounted for but such of that old stock which could be sold was fetching, in some instances, less than half its book value. Worse, by 1911 the works department was underperforming again, and the profitability of the Holt shop was also falling.

Emily Baker decided on firm action, closing the works department as a separate entity and dispensing with the services of Mr Clarke, but it was almost her last involvement with the business, and in April 1912, just a few days before her death, she nominated Rosamond as Chairman of the company. Ros's sisters, Nellie and Maud were appointed Secretaries of the company.

Ros wasted no time in establishing her control of the business. Just a month later she withdrew the appointment of Nellie and Maud as secretaries, and replaced them with

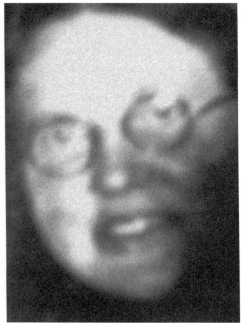

Above left: Aunt Ros, the formidable aunt.

Above right: Aunt Nellie, the vicar's wife.

Above left: Aunt Maud who imigrated to Canada.

Above right: Aunt Mabel, wife of Sir Horace Boot.

herself. The underperformance of the company was becoming evident. A dividend of 25 per cent in 1912 was followed by one of just 10 per cent the following year, and in 1914 the directors felt unable to recommend any dividend at all. This must have been of concern to the shareholders, all of whom attended the meeting at which that decision was made. Blame appears to have been laid at the door of one of the executive directors, Hiram Watson, and at the proposal of Ros he was dismissed from the company and removed from the board. The minutes of the meeting simply referred to 'irregularities which had come to light in connection with his management' and that he 'had been afforded an opportunity for explanation'.

After this the board comprised just two directors, Ros and Mr Scoley, but a month later Maud and Mary (CM's widow) were appointed directors. At the same time Scoley resigned. The first era of the employee/director was over. The company entered the turbulent war period with a status that was probably unique: all the directors and all the shareholders were female.

As chairman and with, just, the largest individual shareholding, Ros ruled the roost. She had moved from Norfolk and her direct oversight was restricted to the occasional visit to Holt. Board meetings were held in London. The directors were entitled to charge rail fares from their normal residence, but were only permitted to charge the third-class fare! The day-to-day management was entrusted to a Mr Hasler and in 1916 a Mr Smith was employed to run the Holt shop. Smith was incentivised in quite a modern way, being offered the choice of a wage of £3 per week plus 5 per cent of the profits of the Holt shop, or a slightly higher wage with smaller profit share.

The shareholders enjoyed a return to growing dividends – they grew each year until they reached 25 per cent in 1920, but then they began to fall again. In the interim, relationships between the four shareholding sisters deteriorated. In 1915 two of them had got married, Nellie to a Suffolk parson named Wilfred Matthews. By contrast Mabel had married Horace (later Sir Horace) Boot, a mechanical engineer and prominent businessman. He was managing director of Eastwoods Ltd, a long-established business primarily concerned with the manufacture of bricks, and a 1934 review of British Industry ascribed to his engineering knowledge and sound commercial judgement, the success of the group of companies he headed.

One might have expected that a man of his background would have been seen as a wonderful asset to the board of a family company which was not performing as well as hoped. Not, apparently, to Ros, who proposed in 1916 that the parson Wilfred should be appointed a director. An amendment, proposed by Mary, that both Wilfred and Horace should join the board was deferred until the next general meeting.

To understand the background to what then happened, two matters need to be considered. First, the distribution of shares at this point was such that while Nellie, Mabel and Maud had each held 1,001 shares, Nellie and Mabel had each transferred two of theirs to their husbands, the transfers being agreed at a board meeting held on Mabel's wedding night – she did not attend the meeting! Mary also held two shares with a further 999 held in trust for her for life. Ros held 1,003.

Second, it is clear that there was already a split between the sisters. A proposal by Mary and Mabel that Ros should be paid £100 per annum for her services as governing director was met with an amendment proposed by Nellie and Maud that she should be paid only half that amount, which was eventually accepted.

When the meeting to determine whether both Horace and Wilfred should join the board took place, the breakdown between the sisters was manifest. The shareholders voted three to two in favour of the amendment, but Nellie insisted on a poll based on the number of votes. The 999 votes held in trust were not voted because the four sisters as Trustees would not have been able to agree on which way to vote. Both Horace and Wilfred voted, and the result was that each side polled 2,002 votes. Ros, as chairman, gave a casting vote against the amendment. As a result the original proposal – to elect just Wilfred to the board – was put to the meeting and rejected by four votes to two. At this, Ros demanded another poll to determine the number of votes, but Wilfred had had enough and withdrew.

One can only speculate as to why Ros seemed determined to keep Horace off the board. The most likely explanation seems to be that she felt threatened by, or at least uncomfortable about, the prospect of the board containing a member with much greater commercial and management experience than herself. Until now she had been able to follow her own devices and desires, but she could well have found her leadership challenged had Horace been on the board too.

By 1918 Mary had resigned as a director, though she was reappointed later. Maud had been unwell and there had not been a quorum at the AGM to approve the accounts. Maud's illness meant it was a propitious time for Ros to try again to elect just Wilfred to the board and sure enough, she did. This time a proposed amendment identified Mabel, rather than her husband to join Wilfred as the new directors. In Maud's absence there were fewer votes available and the amendment was rejected – Maud's votes, if cast as before, would have led to another tie. In this situation there was no means of opposing the sole appointment of Wilfred and, with three abstentions, he was appointed to the board. It would seem that Ros, and Nellie who supported her, suspected that the substitution of Mabel for Horace as an additional director was little more than a sham to enable Horace to intervene by influencing his wife's vote.

The split among the aunts was not confined just to the appointment of additional directors. At the meeting in 1916 when the first vote on the appointment of the new directors was taken, Mabel and Horace, supported by Maud, had also proposed a number of changes to the company's Articles of Association. These were to permit the unfettered transfer of shares, to limit the role of Ros by withdrawing her status as the 'Governing Director', to ensure that, in the case of joint holdings, the votes had to be cast in deference to the wishes of the majority of such joint shareholders, and to authorise each director to have access to a copy of the Report and Accounts. It would seem reasonable to detect the hand of Horace behind the design of these proposed changes. Perhaps Ros was right to be concerned. None of the first three proposals, while each enjoyed a simple majority, attained a sufficient degree of support to permit the proposed amendment to be made, but agreement was reached that each director should be sent a copy of the accounts, within seven days of the AGM. Interestingly it didn't specify that this should be done seven days prior to the AGM, just within seven days of it.

Disputes continued. In 1917 Mabel threatened litigation about property she owned which had been leased to the business, a threat averted by a compromise on terms she

Sir Horace Boot.

dictated. Four years later Horace's persistence identified errors in the calculation of stock, which required a reduction in the proposed dividend. Things were hotting up, and it wasn't long before they boiled over. The aunts divided into two camps, Nellie siding with Ros and Mabel with Maud. When it came down to a vote Ros, Nellie and Wilfred could be sure of winning because of Ros's casting vote.

Something had to give and, as is sometimes the case, the major beneficiaries when it did were the lawyers. There had been discussions about the possibility of the sale of shares, by Mabel to Ros, and by Maud to Nellie. Perhaps Mabel and Maud (and Horace) simply realised that with her casting vote Ros could always win and decided they had had enough. In Ros and Nellie's view those discussions had given rise to a binding agreement as to the sale, and as to the price. Maud and Mabel disagreed and with King's Counsel employed on both sides the matter went to the High Court.

There were two aspects for the court to decide. First, had there been a binding agreement for the sale and purchase of the shares and, if so, whether the valuation of the shares made by the company's auditors constituted a 'fair price', the term which had been used during the original discussions.

Such disputes in family companies are not infrequent, but they are usually inter-generational with the young wanting, as they say in Norfolk, 'to do different'. They tend generally to be resolved without recourse to law, by horse trading within the family.

This dispute was different: the four main protagonists were of the same generation and feelings ran so high that going to law seemed the only option.

By going to court, the dispute became public property and the reporting of the case must have seemed to the family little more than an example of dirty washing being laundered in public. The press duly detailed the decisions made by the court, drawing attention to the dispute having arisen in 'one of the oldest companies in the country' and listing the level of dividends that the shareholders had enjoyed.

The conclusion of the court was in favour of Ros and Nellie, whose counsel argued that as the Articles of Association specified that in the case of a sale of shares the 'fair value' was to be established by the company's auditor who had put a price on the shares of £1.12s.6d each, such should be the price paid. Counsel for Maud and Mabel argued that a fair price was £2. 5s.0d and confirmed that his clients would be willing sellers at that price. His arguments proved to no avail and orders were made for the sale of the shares at the auditor's valuation.

The character of the aunts must have played a part in all these disagreements. Anthony Baker, their great-nephew and the man later responsible for initially organising the effort to keep Baker's a family business, recalls Ros as formidable – very focused and strong willed; to become, as she did, an Alderman in the 1940s in a place as traditional as Royal Tunbridge Wells would have required some strength of character. By contrast he remembers Maud as a far gentler character – although she later lived in Canada, a good relationship persisted. Anthony's father, and then Anthony himself, took care of her affairs in England; she came back to witness Anthony's graduation and he visited her in old age in Canada. The mutual affection, and Maud's Will, were soon to be the saving of Baker's as a genuine family business. Mabel's views almost certainly reflected those of her businessman husband. Anthony recalls her as living in great style near Maidenhead, enjoying the services of butler and footmen. By contrast Nellie may have been concerned most to optimise her income from the shares to augment her husband's stipend.

The result of the case was that Ros and Nellie between them now owned 80 per cent of the shares in the company. Almost all the rest were those held in trust under the terms of Emily Baker's Will. The remaining eight (of 5,007) shares were held by Wilfred, Horace and Mary, each with two, and Mabel and Maud with one apiece, which they may have retained simply out of sentimentality when the rest were sold. As we shall see later the retention of that one share by Maud was going to have a colossal impact on the ownership of the company in years to come. For the moment, though, Maud left the board, married Geoffrey Holt, a Canadian, and went to live the rest of her life in Toronto.

After all the excitement of the court case, things settled down, at least at director level, with Ros, exercising her control at long range, with just the occasional visit to Holt. But what was clear was that, as none of the four sisters had any children, some decisions needed to be made about succession planning.

Of the nephews (the three sons of CM and Mary Baker, equal beneficiaries of her shares under Emily's Will Trust) two, Tom and Jim, were already of age at the time of the court case, and Jacko attained his majority the following year. Of the brothers, Tom had followed his father into the law and Jacko was more interested in horticulture, but Jim joined the business in 1927, and by 1931 was its general manager.

The Nephews

No dividend was declared in 1931, but payments were resumed the following year, albeit at a lower level than before – generally 12 ½ per cent. At this time the business primarily comprised the shops in Holt and Sheringham, a substantial trade in agricultural equipment, a carpenter's shop and a blacksmith. One of the tasks of the carpenter's shop was to make coffins and it was only logical to add undertaking to the range of Baker's businesses. This department offered a special 'perk' – where Baker's acted as undertaker the pall-bearers were required to stand at the back of the church and sing, to supplement the choir, which was itself run by Nellie!

It was not an easy time for Jim to assume his role (in the midst of the depression) yet, except for 1931, a dividend was declared for each year until 1938. Jim was still not a director, the board being again an all-female affair comprising Ros, Nellie and Mary, Jim's mother; it must have been frustrating for him to be answerable to a Tunbridge Wells Alderman, a Suffolk vicar's wife and his own mother. Nonetheless he did negotiate a reward package for himself with an enhanced basic and an escalating percentage of profits. In his role he was assisted by Mr Haslar, who had joined the company during the First World War. Haslar was effectually Jim's deputy, but in 1941 Jim was commissioned in the Royal Army Ordnance Corps and Haslar stood in for him. This proved only a very short-term move because Jim, having suffered a nervous breakdown, was discharged from the army on medical grounds. By 1942 he was not only back but also planning to resign from the company, perhaps frustrated by having a board whose only commercially minded member, Ros, was now not only an even less frequent visitor to Holt because of wartime travel difficulties, but also seemed disinclined to put Jim on the board; her objection may have been an echo of her resistance to Horace Boot's appointment – Jim was running the company and had a far better understanding than she of what made the business tick.

Jim was asked to reconsider his resignation, and at the next board there was discussion as to whether he should be appointed chairman. In fact, Nellie chaired the meeting, having apparently fallen out with Ros, who didn't even attend, citing her 'war work' as making attendance impossible. At the meeting one share was allocated each to Jim and Jacko, these being made available by the recent death of Mabel and by reducing Mary's stake to one share.

By the 1943 meeting Ros was again trying to exercise control remotely. She issued the agenda for the meeting but again failed to attend. Her falling out with Nellie seems confirmed by the latter's proposal that Ros should cease to be a director. This was carried, as was a proposal that Jim should be appointed both a director and chairman. Perhaps the fire in Ros had diminished, or perhaps the memory of the previous court case was too painful, because this time family horse trading did the trick and Ros, somewhat reluctantly, agreed to sell her shares at a price of £2.2s.0d. Despite this she must have

Tom Baker.

Jim Baker.

Jacko Baker.

resented Jim's appointment, their relationship never recovered and they had very little to do with each other in future.

The disposal of Ros's shares left Nellie holding more than 50 per cent of the entire share capital, but with Jim, Tom and, to a lesser extent, Jacko, holding a number of shares. Horace had died by this time so his counsel was not available to Jim when he became chairman as well as managing director – a combination of roles which sometimes causes problems. Jim identified the issues as a lack of capital (a long-term issue for the company) and problems associated with the supply of both labour and material in the war years. His response was to seek to conserve the assets for better times and to buy stock only with the greatest prudence.

By 1946 the problems were compounded because of post-war restrictions, 'our liberty is assailed' he wrote in that year, also referring to the difficulty caused by 'a maze of red tape (which) seems to be in danger of throttling us'. Plus ça change. Despite these difficulties the company made steady progress and consistent dividends were paid throughout the early post-war years, despite a brief and unsuccessful attempt to build a significant agricultural machinery business. The cloud on the horizon was, again, a lack of capital to enable expansion, and the constraints of an overdraft towards the limits of the bank's patience.

Nellie's involvement with the business lessened as she grew older, and after the death of Wilfred in 1950 she arranged to be replaced on the board by her solicitor as her representative until her death in 1955. Nellie, in her will, addressed the issue of equity by so arranging things that the shareholdings of the Jim, Jacko and Tom would be equal.

Unfortunately the three brothers got on with each other little better than the four aunts who preceded them. It would not be surprising if Jim, who had spent thirty years working in the business, felt hard done by when his brothers, who had not, were equal shareholders with him. On the other hand, Tom and Jacko could see that Jim was spending time on his other interests, particularly his farm. Further he was in debt to the company.

There were problems within the business, too. The apparently perennial problems of high customer debt provisions and poor stock recording compounded those caused as the bank pressed for a reduction of the overdraft. In 1953 the shop in Sheringham had been closed, the company receiving £1,000 as compensation for the early termination of its lease, to be spent on improving the condition of the Holt retail premises.

By 1958 the tensions between the brothers were such that Jim was replaced as chairman, by Tom. Two years earlier a Mr Scott had been appointed as assistant manager to help resolve these issues and was quickly appointed to the board on his purchase of 156 newly issued shares, for which he paid £3.04s.3d each. Scott was friendly with another businessman, J. G. Camroux, who had moved to Norfolk and was the owner of premises next door to the Holt shop. On Scott's introduction he was also appointed a director, and took on a salaried management role within the company. The only firm clue to the reasons for his appointment lies in his ownership of adjoining premises, which may have offered the opportunity for a new joint venture. The appointment does seem to have been driven by Scott – one can only speculate on his motives.

In 1960 Jim died suddenly, and thus no member of the family was left with executive responsibility within the company. His death brought about, for the first time, a circumstance in which a large parcel of shares were held outside the family. The company's articles provided that, on the death of any executive director, his shares could be bought by other directors. Jim's shares were snapped up by Mr Camroux at just £2 per share, a price hotly disputed by Jim's executors. With the exception of that single share (now actually four, following a bonus issue) owned by Maud, all shares were now held by directors of the company. Camroux seems to have been a dominant force in the running of the company, being appointed secretary in 1970, and in 1972 he welcomed an approach for the sale of the business as a whole. He was supported both by Scott and Jacko, and less enthusiastically by Tom.

This was the point at which Maud's shares became critical. She had died in 1968, leaving those shares to Jim's son, Anthony. The directors had immediately sought to stop the shares being registered as Anthony's as they wished all the shares to be in their own hands. They were unable to do so, and because of his shareholding Anthony received advance warning of the proposal to sell out. He was thus able to attend the meeting at which the directors decided to open negotiations for the sale.

Anthony was only one of the members of the next generation and was so concerned by the proposal that he discussed it informally with his cousins, Miles and Michael. They shared his concern and at the next meeting Anthony was able to persuade the other shareholders to allow the three cousins to make alternative proposals while the negotiations were under way.

Anthony Baker's graduation, 1955, with his mother and sister, and, to his left, aunt Maud who, by leaving him her shares, enabled the business to remain in the family.

Prompt action was needed if the company were to remain in family hands and the three met without delay to discuss what to do. Happily this generation, unlike the previous ones, was able to work together in a degree of harmony. Two conclusions arose from the meeting. First, all three wanted to see the company remain in family hands. Second, this could only work if at least one of them became involved in an executive capacity.

The Concordat of Cousins

Anthony had followed the other family tradition and was a successful London solicitor with no retail aspirations. Miles, married with a young family and pursuing a career in the motor industry, did not want to change course. Michael, by far the youngest, was working in an uncongenial role as a chemical engineer and was willing to take on the task. The next step was to persuade the older generation to change their minds about the disposal. As we have seen, Tom had been the least enthusiastic about the proposal and quickly came round to the idea. Michael, Jacko's son, was able to persuade his father to reconsider too, and at the next board meeting Tom, as chairman, advised the meeting that he and Jacko had decided that they were only prepared to consider a sale to members of the family.

That single share (four after the bonus issue) of Maud's acquired by Anthony had totally changed the situation, and Camroux, frustrated, indicated that he was willing to sell his shares, albeit asking a price which failed to take account of the changed position. In fact there was no immediate prospect of the availability of capital for the young Turks to buy the non-family-held shares.

Not for the first time, the board was less than unanimous. A proposal that Anthony and Miles should be appointed to the board was postponed, and Michael's appointment as Scott's assistant was resisted by both Camroux and Scott, but carried on Tom's casting vote as chairman. Their resistance cannot have made it easy for Michael, but he started in his new role immediately.

He quickly came to the conclusion that the company was being badly managed and his view was accepted by Tom and Jacko. At the next meeting Tom revisited the proposal to appoint Anthony and Miles as directors, and indicated that he was prepared to use his casting vote to ensure its acceptance. This proved unnecessary, the proposal being accepted. The reinforced board, in 1974, moved swiftly and decisively, appointing Michael as a director, and terminating Scott's employment, only Scott himself arguing against the proposition. Although the board 'recorded its gratitude' to Scott, it seems clear that Michael had quickly reached the conclusion that he had not been managing effectively. Michael was appointed as managing director and soon afterwards reported more fully on the state of the business. The board decided also to terminate Mr Camroux's employment, and he and Mr Scott were left as minority shareholders. Both decided to resign from the board and a brisk negotiation took place over the sale of their shares, which were acquired by family members, mainly Anthony, at reasonable cost. The board now comprised only family members and the shares were all now equally held by the three branches of the family.

Most importantly, the good relationship between family members continued – perhaps the memory of the infighting great aunts and the disagreements between their nephews

Anthony Baker.

Miles Baker.

Michael Baker.

who succeeded them was warning enough. The new generation determined on a plan to ensure that cooperation continued. Michael was guaranteed the role of managing director for ten years; Miles was offered the option of sharing that role at a time of his own choosing within the following decade, and Anthony the option of becoming finance director. Mindful of the arguments of the preceding generations they each agreed not to acquire a majority shareholding without the consent of the others. They had the discipline to enshrine these agreements in a legally binding deed, and the wit to agree that there should always be a director who was not a member of the family, thus ensuring at least one independent voice.

With the combination of this new-found family solidarity and Michael's energy and flair applied to the task, an era began when Baker's started to earn the iconic status it enjoys today.

In its long history the company had managed to navigate some stormy patches in terms of the external economy and environment despite a series of internal arguments. Insufficient commercial experience within the family had necessitated the employment of external managers. Now with a strong commitment to the maintenance of good relations between the shareholders and a member of the family with both the commercial nous and the energy of youth as managing director the old failings could be addressed.

Still, in the mid-1970s, walking into the shop was described by Michael as like walking back into the nineteenth century. Purchasers had to take their purchase and a docket to a central cash desk and pay the cashier, whose raised dais was reached only after negotiating worn floorboards with holes disguised by the use of pieces of tin. Baker's also collected money for Holt's gas bills – residents brought in their cash which was stored, pending transmission, in an Oxo tin under the cashier's feet to keep the money separate from that for purchases in the shop. Transmission of the cash to the gas board apparently sometimes only happened when an angry customer who had paid weeks before came into the shop with the 'red reminder' he had received. The premises themselves were in such disrepair that heavy rain meant the immediate despatch of a staff member to the attic to place the twenty buckets kept there ready where they were most needed. So niggardly had been the amount spent on maintenance that it was difficult to get local firms to do necessary work – builders were hesitant even to do simple tile replacement because of the danger involved; it was rumoured that any local firm which accepted a contract to work on the premises did so only because they were in debt to the store.

And that reinforced another impression. The old bugbear of bad credit control was as big an issue as ever. Very little effort had been made to collect long-term debt. This seems to have been something of a Holt tradition. The author (whose family moved to Holt in the late 1940s) recalls his parents' frustration with another Holt retailer who had to be asked repeatedly to provide an account for goods supplied. It was very rare for that particular shop to issue bills less than a year after they became due! Such delay may have helped domestic budgets, but it did nothing for those of the business and things had to be tightened up – the new broom quickly got himself known as he collected the amounts owed. The company had concluded that pursuing debtors through the courts was expensive and slow and that a direct approach, with the threat of court back-up worked better. Another example of the chaotic accounts process Michael discovered occurred when a beet hoe was sold to a local farmer, but not booked to his account. The solution was to bill the item to no less than twelve possible purchasers – all twelve paid off the account!

The other long-term problem of stock order, valuation, and control was still to be resolved too. Mr Scott had been in the habit of deciding, for example, whether to buy more copper tube on the basis of his own interpretation of the trend in commodity prices rather than to reflect customer demand. Stock control was chaotic: purchasers usually found that Baker's did stock what they wanted but had to waste precious hours while the staff tried to find where the object was stored. There was a standing joke that if buying at Baker's the customer should take a book to occupy the time it took to locate the goods he had bought. The solution was to reform the basis of internal stock valuations and take a less optimistic attitude to old or unsaleable stock.

As these long-term problems were resolved, new challenges arose – the economy had suffered grievously, both from the Heath government's war of attrition with the miners and the three-day week it imposed, and then by the massive inflation under the Labour government, which peaked at 26 per cent. The chosen weapon to deal with this was to raise interest rates – at peak the minimum bank lending rate reached a level thirty-one times that pertaining in 2015. Such conditions were hardly conducive to profitable retailing and the board decided that to survive the company needed to invest in expanding and improving its retail premises. This proved a major task: extensive areas proved to be affected by dry rot but the work was carried out so well as to be rewarded with a conservation award.

Wanting to extend even further, the owner of the adjoining Larners store (on the site sold by Charles Baker more than a century before) was approached with a view to selling the business to Bakers, and after some hesitation (and haggling) agreed. It was to be the first of a number of acquisitions which, combined with the organic growth of the business, was to turn a fairly small company into one with an annual turnover nudging £24 million by 2014. The acquisition of Larners, a long-established, if financially strapped, draper, grocer and wine merchant, afforded both challenges and opportunities. The main challenge was financial – regaining the confidence of suppliers who had been waiting long and, until now, in vain, for the settlement of their accounts, was a costly business. On the other hand, wine was to become a major offering of the enlarged group. Michael was an enthusiast, who rapidly added deep professional knowledge, gaining a succession of qualifications from the Wine and Spirit Education Trust. Visiting Bakers extensive cellars in his company today is to witness a true love affair, especially in the area reserved for vintage port. It is difficult to believe that these immaculately kept cellars, under the former Larner's premises, were the site of some of the worst dry rot. Selling some, and leasing other, parts of the former Larners premises helped to meet the cost of rebuilding.

Not all acquisitions were as successful. Expansion by purchasing businesses away from Holt – a wine store on the outskirts of Norwich for example – were not always as happy, but even these did not deter the company from more acquisitions, though in the retail arena it encouraged a strategy of focussing on local businesses. In 2003 the purchase of the menswear and ladies fashion business, Betty's of Holt was achieved. Betty's was a business owned by Baker's major North Norfolk rivals, Aldiss of Fakenham. Four years later Baker's acquired the Budgen's supermarket in Holt, subject to the stipulation that it would trade under the Budgen's name for a term of twenty years. Soon it added the sister store in Aylsham.

Michael Baker with his stock of vintage port in the cellars of his store.

In both cases, another strand of the Baker strategy was brought to bear – one of adapt and improve. Betty's fashion departments moved into Baker's main store leaving their former premises available for the furniture department. Budgens in Holt underwent a facelift which greatly enhanced its appeal – just as well given the competitive nature of the supermarket business and the threat posed by new competitors with a purely price driven proposition. In addition to all this Bakers rapidly grew a separate business as Builders' Merchants, though that is a separate story. By diversifying in this way the company has been able to reduce the risk to its core business in the event of recession in the retail sector.

By 2014 Bakers and Larners had a turnover more than 130 times that when Anthony, Miles and Michael stepped in to prevent the sale of the business. In the same period the staff had grown from 17 to 296. Those employees are critical to the continued success of the company and this is recognised in the establishment of a profit-sharing scheme which entitles staff members to share 5 per cent of the net profits each year.

This remarkable growth has been achieved despite the early death of Miles and of his son Tom who had succeeded him, and is a tribute not just to the drive of the seventh generation of Bakers involved in the business, but also to their wisdom in garnering non-executive directors with commercial skills. First, in 1977 they appointed to the board Gordon Youngs, who had recently retired as a partner in the accountancy practice of their auditors. On his retirement in 1986 Antony introduced an acquaintance, E. E. Ray, then senior partner at the well-known London practice of Spicer and Pegler, who was planning to retire to North Norfolk and agreed to become a non-executive director. Mr Ray was obviously a perceptive man. Apparently, when invited to join the board he first enquired as to whether there was a family dispute to resolve. For the first time in three generations the honest answer could be 'No'. At this stage Anthony chaired the board, but his son Malcolm, a chartered accountant, had been appointed to the board as a member of the eighth generation. It wasn't long before he decided to approach his father, and suggest that he stand down as chairman in favour of Mr Ray. The seventh generation thus had the benefit of sound considered advice to temper any over exuberance which they might have otherwise exhibited, and had learned the value of having at least one independent director – perhaps not before time. They later appointed a non-family executive director, Jane Gurney-Read, who had previously worked for Debenhams. Malcolm became chairman in 2013, and Miles's son Nicholas was already on the board, so the eighth generation from two branches of the family continue to be involved. Under Michael's management there has been a string of initiatives to keep the business prosperous. To leverage the delicatessen the range has been extended to include fine pre-prepared meals and luxury hampers; regular tastings, of food, of wine and of specialist teas and coffees have been introduced. This emphasis on developing this personal contact with customers is key to the Baker philosophy in respect of its traditional market. But other markets require a different approach and Bakers were early users of the internet. Their strategy for online business with this mechanism is well differentiated. Instead of the discounting policy adopted by many, Baker's take the opportunity to distribute the eclectic range of goods in their delicatessen far beyond the confines of North Norfolk. Michael Baker quotes an example of a recent order for a specialist tea from a lady in Singapore. The order was received on a Thursday and within three days the customer had emailed the store to say how much she was enjoying her tea! Not all orders are for the delicatessen though; one early internet sale was of twenty-four footballs, ordered by a prominent citizen of Kazakhstan! Today Bakers are looking to harness the power of social media to ensure that they are able to appeal not just to their traditional market but to new ones as well.

The story of the company is a romantic one. Its modest eighteenth-century beginnings, its nineteenth-century growth in the face of a severe agricultural depression, its twentieth-century shenanigans with the gaggle of aunts and the brothers who could agree on so little make it so. The romance is enhanced by more recent events – the seventh generation determined not to repeat the infighting of previous generations, Michael gladly surrendering his professional career and flying back to Holt on his magic carpet, first to sort out the underperformance issues and then to move rapidly into a period of growth – an opportunity only available because Aunt Maud left her originally single share to Anthony. It's the stuff of television mini-drama, but for real.

If John Baker were to be whisked back to his store by a time machine he would barely recognise anything, but one can be confident that he would be very proud of what his descendants have achieved. He would have been pleased too at the determination they have shown both to keep the business in the family, and to eschew the tradition of disagreement among some of the intervening generations. It might though have taken even the articulate Michael Baker some time to explain to his great-great-great-great-grandfather how an eighteenth-century country ironmonger came to be supplying twenty-first-century footballs to Kazakhstan!

Michael Baker outside his store with his celebratory banner.

Break's Chain of Charity Shops

An expanding empire of shops that help to 'change young lives', by contributing more than £1,000,000 each year to the work of the Norfolk based charity.

Every Dot is a Break Shop

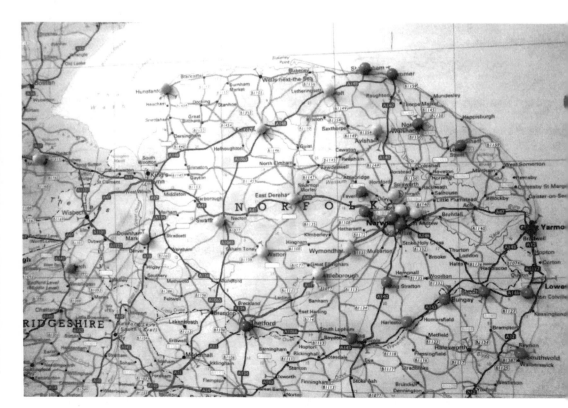

Location of Break shops in Norfolk.

It seemed a normal autumn day in 2009. In the doorway of Break's shop in Holt was the usual assortment of black bin bags, full of discarded goods donated by members of the public for sale by the charity. The manager, Sue Billings, opened up the shop and started the daily task of tipping up the bags so that the contents could be sorted, expecting the usual haul of a mixture of clothes, books, pictures, glass and chinaware. One of the sacks was unusually heavy and she felt inside the bag to discover the cause. She was astonished and shocked to pull out two pistols – very frightening as Holt is in East Anglia not the Wild West. Sue promptly phoned the police, worried that by removing the guns she had left her own fingerprints on them. The police were quickly on the scene and were able to tell her that the pistols were in fact replicas but high-quality ones of the type sometimes used to frighten victims of crime. Fortunately there turned out to be no recorded incident involving missing replicas of that kind and they were destroyed by the police without Sue having to explain away the presence of her fingerprints.

Not all donated goods are so alarming, but the characteristic that distinguishes Break's shops from all the others in this book is that it has no need, or opportunity, to decide what it will stock – it can only sell what it is given. It may seem strange, in a book which has been all about family run department stores, to include a chapter on a totally different kind of retailer, one which is run not for profit but to generate income to meet charitable ends. Yet despite the huge differences there is one great similarity. Arnold Roy's claim to sell anything from 'a pin to an elephant' applies just as much to a chain of charity shops as it does to a department store; it can include, literally, the kitchen sink. On one occasion a volunteer in the Holt shop, Shaun Rendle-Hunt, discovered that while he had been serving a customer someone had come into the shop and left there an old sink, complete with taps. Sadly its condition was so poor that it had to be taken to the tip.

Break is a Norfolk-based charity going back nearly fifty years and has proved itself an effective retailer, so much so that it now has fifty-two shops, around thirty of them in Norfolk. In the early days the charity provided holiday breaks for children who were disabled or disadvantaged, and it has, in more recent times, undertaken a much extended range of activities, from providing homes for children in care to involvement with the development of parenting skills and the undertaking of assessments to enable better decisions to be made about the best way to care for children in difficult circumstances. One particular facet of Break's work, and a very important one, is the development of its 'Moving On' programme, designed to help youngsters achieving adulthood make the change from being 'looked after' in a home to establishing themselves in the outside adult world. This part of their work depends entirely on charitable giving, and this is where Break's retail chain plays a vital part.

In recent years these shops have generated a net annual contribution to charitable funds in excess of £1,000,000. Although one-off fundraising events also make a huge contribution, the especial value of the retail income is its consistency, which enables planned investment in those leaving care. Lesley Leigh, Break's retail business manager first became involved with the charity as a volunteer, but twenty-two years ago she joined the staff and moved up through the ranks to her present role. Reporting to the deputy chief executive, she is the key figure in determining what retail strategy should be proposed to the board. In recent years this strategy has been one of targeted growth. The first shop was opened in 1968, but the numbers have grown dramatically in the last few years when the plan has been to open three new shops a year, a target which has been achieved. Openings

Lesley Leigh in Break's Holt shop.

'Captain Hook' opens a Norwich shop.

are usually undertaken by a local celebrity, but on one occasion a new shop in Norwich was opened by a supporter 'dressed' as Lady Godiva! On another, Break's handyman for eighteen years, Peter Dormer, put in an appearance dressed as Captain Hook to the amusement of local children.

Lesley explains 'a period of recession works both for and against us. While many people will not replace goods so frequently – which has a negative effect on levels of stock, adverse economic conditions also help us in that more retail premises become available, and at more reasonable rents'. Because Break targets particular locations which it believes will prove sustainable both in terms of acquiring and selling stock, it can take a long-term view; it is there to stay. Generally it will seek premises where a nine- to twelve-year lease is available at a rent which allows an expectation of a reasonable return.

Opening new branches is hard going – funds are not wasted employing professional shopfitters. Most of the work of converting and fitting the premises is carried out by Break's own staff, and even the retail business manager is not exempt, seen here decorating the Sheringham shop. Peter Dormer, now retired but still working, with his wife, as a volunteer in Break shops was, before he retired, largely responsible for the preparation and conversion of new premises with plenty of 'hands-on' encouragement from Lesley and before that from Break's previous director of fundraising, Rosemary Fereday, in whose time the expansion of the shop empire began.

Some new shops provided particular challenges. One, in Carlton Colville, had previously been a café – before the shop could open Peter had to remove all the cooking and other equipment, knock down the wall which had divided the large food preparation area from

Lesley Leigh helping to prepare the Break shop at Sheringham.

the dining one, and build a new wall to separate the retail area from the administration – a big task for one man. On another occasion he was sent to Yeovil to prepare premises for a new shop – a job scheduled to take a week. But the condition of the premises was so poor that it took a fortnight. Fortunately there had already been donations to the shop of an iron and board, so, having used the neighbouring launderette he set the gifts up and made himself presentable for the unplanned second week.

In difficult economic times, despite the downturn in donated stock, there are some advantages for a charity shop. Running costs are modest, not just in terms of stock but in staffing costs too. Each shop is managed by just one full-time and one part-time employee. Most of those working in the shops are volunteers – no less than 900 of them. Without the generosity of all these people, some giving just a few hours but many giving more, the retail arm of the charity would not be viable. Some of those volunteers have helped in the shops for thirty years or more, and they have some fascinating tales to tell. When sacks of good are left in a shop doorway, there is no knowing what haul they will yield.

Most donations, and generally the best-selling, are ladies clothes. One task of the volunteers is to steam clean every item of clothing which is going to be sold – sometimes parts of the shop feel more like a sauna. Not all the donations are sold in the shop, but it is a feature of this kind of business that a turn can be taken on just about everything. Clothing not suitable for shop resale is bundled up and sold for rags, and good prices can be obtained for metal sold on for salvage. Just about everything is welcomed, except televisions where the responsibility for notifying licensing authorities makes the administrative burden unacceptable. Being a local charity, and one which operates a number of children's homes, Break has its own maintenance team who test and certify all electrical goods sold in the shops.

The range of goods offered can be surprising; sometimes there is an unexpected bonus. Recently a pair of jeans donated at one shop and later transferred to another yielded a haul of £40 found in a pocket when the garment was cleaned. On another occasion a box anonymously donated was found to contain £1,000 in cash. Here the money was handed into the police station as a 'found item' but the donor did not claim the money which then was added to the charitable funds.

Sometimes money can be raised without any sale. On one occasion a rather embarrassed man entered one shop carrying a brand-new and expensive tweed jacket together with a brand-new shirt. 'Will you sell me two Break labels?' he asked. 'Yes' the manager replied. 'Can you attach them to the shirt and jacket for me?' Again, 'yes'. At this point he obviously decided that he should explain his strange request. It turned out that he was going to a stag party at which it was a requirement that guests must wear clothes bought at a charity shop and he had to 'prove' to his friends that he had done so, despite being unwilling to wear second-hand goods.

On another occasion a lady carefully went through all the racks and chose a whole armful of clothes which she brought to the counter. Suddenly a realisation came to her: 'Is this a second-hand shop' she asked. 'I can't possibly buy second-hand', and she left the goods and ran. Her confusion is understandable. Some charity shops do sell new clothes, obtained as a result of, for example, the willingness of a manufacturer effectively to 'remainder' large amounts of unsold stock. Break does not engage in this practice. 'Our

Four volunteers at the Holt shop with a total of 100 years of service. From left to right: Ghisline Kindley, Madeleine Lutwieler, Geraldine Watson and Joy Wright.

relationship with other retailers is important to us' says Lesley, 'to take up offers of new garments at knock down prices would not be fair to them'.

Stock is turned over fast. One of the favourite stories is that of the lady customer who, when trying on an article of clothing, first removed her coat. Delighted with the appearance of her new garment she left the shop, forgetting first to collect her coat. By the time she remembered an hour or so later, and returned to the shop, the coat had been sold, innocently enough, by an assistant who just thought it was a new piece of stock.

The shops aim to have clothes which are donated checked, cleaned, priced and back on the floor on the same day they are received, or the day after. Sue Billings explained how the process works at Holt. First it is necessary to establish whether the item is of sufficiently good quality to sell in the shop. It is then steam cleaned and Sue, in conjunction with her relief manager, determines at what price it should be sold. The key is consistency: the price needs to reflect not just the condition but the original value. 'We have three basic price ranges' explains Sue, 'one for clothes which were inexpensive originally, another for middle of the road garments, and a third for those which carry a fashionable designer label. For example, we would price garments in similar condition more expensively with a Gerry Weber label than one originally from M & S.' And it's not just ladies clothing that Break sells. When the charity held a special dinner and charity auction at Holkham Hall both the recently retired chief executive and the current deputy chief executive wore dinner jackets they had bought in Break shops. On a number of occasions Break has held

A wedding fashion show at the Aylsham shop.

fashion parades in its shops – a means not just of showing off its wares but a source itself of additional income to the charity, as on this occasion at Aylsham in 2003.

Optimising the income from all these donations is the key to making such a large contribution to the charitable funds. Managers have to be aware. Sometimes items are donated which have a value beyond what could be achieved in the High Street. Managers are trained to be alert to special opportunities, such as the rare first edition which brought £700 at auction, or the pair of vases, originally destined for the rubbish bin because of their condition, which the manager stepped in and saved; they fetched £800 at auction. Stock is moved around between branches. Part of Lesley's role is to identify what sort of item will sell best in each shop. 'Men with vans' have been recruited and continually move stock either to where it is likely to sell best or to shops where the quantity of donated items has fallen short of the shop's capacity to sell. The managers have responsibility for pricing new items of stock. Sue Billings explains that over her eleven years in the shop at Holt she has built up a network of local experts who freely give their advice on the pricing of items such as books, pictures and jewellery. Often these are the owners of local businesses, and that anxiety on Lesley Leigh's part to develop good relationships with local shops helps in this.

At the time when the writer was chairman of Break he was privileged to visit a number of the shops, learning a lot about their role from the managers and having an opportunity to thank some of the volunteers for their efforts. He felt a special affinity with the shop in Holt, and not for any charitable feeling. When sweet rationing finally finished in February 1953, as a small boy he splurged in celebration at his local sweet shop, run by an extremely kind spinster called Miss Hall. Today it is Break that occupies what was Miss Hall's sweet shop and sometimes it still sells confectionery. Recently there was a donation comprising an edible G string and a matching posing pouch, both made of small candy sweets. They sold quickly, but Sue Billings's discretion is absolute – she declined to name the purchaser. What the writer is sure of is that the sweet and lovely Miss Hall would have been shocked to the core to be asked to stock such items. Other bizarre items recently offered for sale include a single courgette, a set of false teeth and a pop-up version of the Kama Sutra! On one occasion in North Walsham handyman Peter Dormer had to enlist the help of police in holding up traffic as his van blocked off a narrow road as he single-handedly unloaded a donated piano. He was just glad, he said, that he had not been around when the piano was sold and had to be moved again.

It's not just pricing and selling stock that is the responsibility of the individual shops. In order to make the best possible returns, those donors who can be identified are sometimes asked whether they are willing for the price obtained by the shop to be treated as a charitable donation under the Gift Aid rules. These do not allow items to be given, only cash, so in such cases Break undertakes to sell the item as the donor's agent and then to advise them of the price obtained. At this point they are asked whether they are prepared to donate this sum, and to complete a Gift Aid declaration. With the average item price only £2.50, this may seem a tortuous procedure, but in the average month it makes an additional contribution of £16,000.

Sometimes additional income is achieved in the most unexpected way. Swaffham is a fine mid-Norfolk market town with a beautiful Buttercross, a splendid church, a Georgian

Assembly Room and a collection of fine buildings. Its citizens were perhaps surprised to wake up one morning in 2008 and find that a new sex shop, 'Tiger Lily's', had sprung up overnight, apparently taking over the premises previously occupied by the Break shop in the town. Any consternation would have been short-lived though: it transpired that the makers of the television series Kingdom starring Stephen Fry and Celia Imrie had reached an agreement with the charity to lease the shop while shooting a scene. Soon things got back to normal, with the goods on offer becoming rather less exotic. Break's charitable funds had received a welcome boost. Even the writer's rusty Latin (dormant since a scraped 'O' Level pass c 1960) tells him that while the sign used by the shop in the programme only omits one letter of the summation of the philosophy of Descartes. The end result is a clever, if rather naughty, pun changing the meaning significantly!

In order to optimise as far as possible the value of the gifts donated some are differentiated from the rest. Items that can be described as 'vintage', whether clothes or any kind of artefact, are in some cases sold through a special 'vintage' shop. Identifying the best site for this kind of specialisation has been achieved by experimenting in different areas – the location that emerged as the most appropriate was Tewkesbury. One other specialisation has been wedding apparel where Holbeach has proved the best choice. Some goods are not sold in the shops at all; where the opportunity for profit seems higher elsewhere alternative routes will be taken. Obviously some high-value items are best put up for conventional auction, but eBay is a medium which is used as well. The whole process is geared to maximising the amount available for charitable use and the choice

A memento presented to Break by the cast of *Kingdom*.

The motto of Tiger Lily's temporary sex shop at Break's Swaffham shop.

of whether to sell over the counter, online or by auction is just one of the matters of judgement which characterises the role of managing a chain of charity shops.

Even though there is no purchasing of stock, Break's shops are in other ways as demanding to manage as any of the other retailers described in this book. Indeed with more than twenty shops out of county, many in the West Country, management is in some ways more difficult, especially in terms of warehousing stock and moving it to the most suitable selling site. The existence of shops in the West reflects a bit of history: in the early days Break recruited someone from the area to set up its first retail outlets. He was unable to move East as originally intended and instead set to work establishing Break's presence there. Later a strategic decision was taken to stay with those original shops, which were doing very well, if enough other sites could be found to build a significant regional presence. Today the out of county shops make a major contribution and the whole network is managed through a team of area managers who report to Lesley.

The achievements of Break's retail team are well understood and appreciated by the senior management and trustees. The contribution made by the shops is an extremely important part of the charity's fund raising activities and in the hands of a team with such a track record of success it seems certain that it will remain so. More shops will almost certainly follow.

About the Author

Chris Armstrong was born and bred in Norfolk, but spent nearly thirty years working elsewhere, most of it trying to find a way back! For the last twenty-five years he has lived near Holt.

His previous books, *Under the Parson's Nose* and *Mustard, Boots and Beer* were published by Larks Press in 2012 and 2014, respectively.

When not enjoying Norfolk he is usually to be found adding to his already extensive collection of Test Match grounds around the world on which he has witnessed an English batting collapse.